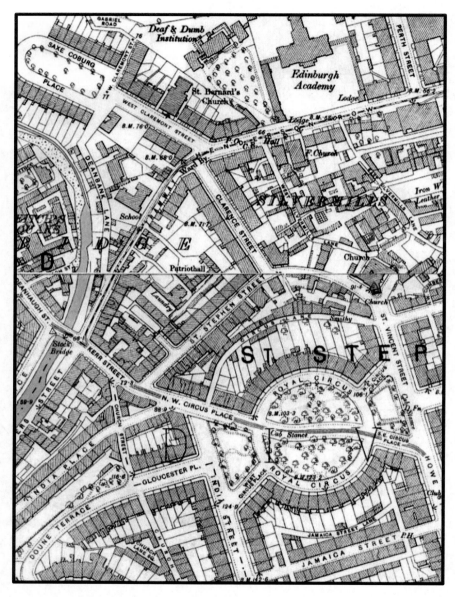

Detail from Ordnance Survey 1894 (National Library of Scotland)

A History of
St Stephen Street

Barclay Price

© 2022

CONTENTS

1. St Stephen Street, c. 1910
2. St Stephen Street, c. 1970 (photo - Jon Christophersen)
3. St Stephen Street, 2022

Introduction

It was around 200 years ago that the building of St Stephen Street began, and since then the street's fortunes have waned and waxed. Fifty years ago the street was threatened with demolition but thanks to those who fought to save it, today is a vibrant community and tourist destination. Any 200-year-old street is bound to contain a myriad of stories and this book can only scratch the surface of St Stephen Street's fascinating history.

My earlier history of Albany Street managed to provide information on the majority of that street's residents but this is not feasible for St Stephen Street, as thousands have passed through its many tenement flats. Instead I have chosen two tenements and by tracing the lives of a number of the occupants provide a partial portrait of the changing nature of those who lived in the street through to the 1920s.

I have trawled widely for relevant images and apologise if I have failed to provide due credit for any. As the book is being produced in short runs, any missing credits can be easily inserted by contacting me. Similarly, I would welcome feedback on any inaccuracies or other comments. Thanks for help and content to the Facebook pages of Lost Scotland and Peter Stubbs' website, EdinPhoto – both packed with great Edinburgh memories. Also to Fiona and Oula for proof-reading, and Oula for creating the index.

Barclay Price
Contact email: albanystreeetedinburgh@gmail.com

About the author

After retiring from working in the arts Barclay Price developed an interest in local history research. See page 127 for his other books linked to the history of the city. His book, *The Chinese In Britain – A History of Visitors and Settlers*, stemmed from his discovery that the first Chinese man to settle in Britain lived and worked in Edinburgh from the 1770s to 1831, and the story of his remarkable life forms one chapter of that book.

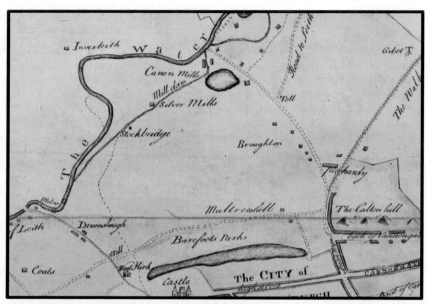

1. 1759 map showing the village of Stockbridge by Richard Cooper (National Library of Scotland)

2. Old bridge, c.1750

3

Building the street

Until the mid-18th century Stockbridge was a separate entity from Scotland's capital city, just one of several isolated villages that formed a constellation around Edinburgh. Much of the land originally belonged to George Heriot's Hospital (school), which had been given it by Charles I in 1636 in lieu of money owed. In 1712 the Hospital advertised land for early development: 'The Council intend to feu the Mills of Stockbridge, with the ground lying about the same commonly called the Midlands, and the Grass-brae lying to the south-west of same inclosures. Any person who inclines to feu the same, may give in signed proposals to David Flint, Treasurer.' This led to the building of a number of country houses in the area and also the construction of a mill lade (artificial millstream) that channelled water from Dean Village to Canon Mills Loch. The mill lade allowed a range of industries to be established in the Silvermills area that by 1815 included a flour mill, a tannery, blacksmith's shops, a yarn wash-house, a large distillery, a skinner's workshop and a sawmill.

The original road - Stockbridge Brae – that led from the village up to the city was steep and bounded by hawthorn hedges on which the local women 'were wont to dry their clothes.' In 1743 the population of Stockbridge Village was recorded as being just over 500.

By the 18th century Edinburgh had become the most densely populated city in Europe and whilst this overcrowding created a dynamic that helped drive the new ideas of the Edinburgh Enlightenment, many of the wealthy citizens no longer felt the outdated city fabric suitable for modern living. Concerned at the prospect of influential citizens leaving Edinburgh, the city decided to construct the New Town on the fields to the north of the Nor Loch. In 1766 a design competition was held to find a suitably modern layout for the new suburb, which was won by the 26-year-old James Craig.

Significant demand for properties in the New Town led to an enlargement of the original Craig plan and development moved down the hill towards Stockbridge. The vision for the New Town had been to create townhouses with a country feel and the romantic glen created by the Water of Leith to the west of Stockbridge fitted perfectly with that aspiration.

The appeal of the area was enhanced in the mid-18th century, when St Bernard's Well became reputed for its medicinal qualities, and the nobility and gentry visited to drink the water, In 1788 Lord Gardenstone, a wealthy Court of Session judge who thought he had benefited from the mineral spring, commissioned the architect, Alexander Nasmyth to design a new pump room. His circular Greek temple supported by ten tall Doric order columns was built by John Wilson and in 1791 a statue of Hygieia, the Greek goddess of health, was added. The pump room contains a splendid

1. View of Stockbridge looking north, 1786
2. View of Stockbridge looking south, 1825
3. Advert for sale of the feus, 1741
4. Sir Henry Raeburn, self-portrait, c.1820

mosaic interior by Thomas Bonnar. 'Bernard's Well has long been celebrated for its wonderful powers in all diseases of the eyes, herpetic eruptions, and dyspeptic complaints, or what are ordinarily called indigestion and diseases of the stomach, weak and lax fibres, asthma, scorbutic and scrofulous eruptions, &c. The water is impregnated with sulphurated hydrogen gas, and holds carbonate of lime in solution. Few mineral springs in the United Kingdom have proved more efficacious in the prevention and cure of those numerous diseases to which the human frame is liable. The walk to Bernard's Well is short and pleasant, by Stockbridge, and it is of the utmost importance to the health of the inhabitants of the city of Edinburgh to be made better acquainted with it. Bottles sent to the well must be sufficiently corked, and the keeper will place a seal of St Bernard's Well on all bottles and packages which contain water. Numerous cases of cures can be seen at the well.'

Those who visited Stockbridge to partake of the effervescent waters in the early 19th century may have come across one of the village's characters, Barclay Reddie. 'He was very irritable and furious when provoked, and always carried a large stick, which he used freely on the shoulders of his tormentors when they came within his reach. He was an old man, and in general very dirty and greasy looking. The celebrated painter Henry Raeburn who owned the Stockbridge estates of Deanhaugh and St Bernard's was very kind to him. He went every day to St Bernard's for his dinner. On one occasion when Barclay had been ill used, Sir Henry wrote out a hand-bill and had it posted upon one of the conical shaped stones at the bridge, offering a reward of ten shillings to anyone who would give information as to the guilty party. He was dressed in Sir Henry's old clothes, and generally put on a coat just as he got it. Sir Henry being tall and Barclay rather short, the tails of the coat nearly touched the ground. Barclay died of cholera at its first visit in 1832.'

Owners of land began to develop the area for profit. In 1801 Raeburn, whose land was on the north side, commissioned a stone bridge to replace the old wooden structure and by 1820 house building was well underway. Robert Chambers, later a partner with his brother William in the book publishing firm of W. & R. Chambers, opened his first Circulating Library in India Place (now 35/37 N. W. Circus Place) across the road from St Stephen's Street and he described the area in his 1825 book, *Walks in Edinburgh*: 'Farther to the west lies Stockbridge which gives name to a sort of village, now surrounded, and partly destroyed, by the encroaching limits of the rapidly-extending city. The glen here formed by the Water of Leith was, till lately, a beautiful and sequestered natural scene; but its echoes, which formerly answered only to the melody of birds and the fall of waters, are now disturbed by the rude sound of the mechanic's hammer,

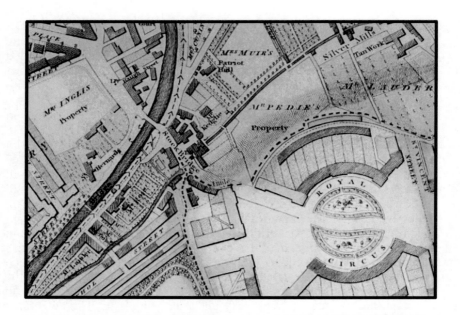

1. James Pedie's land next to the mill lade- detail from 1821 map by James Kirkwood
(National Library of Scotland)
2. Advert by James Pedie offering land for sale, 1823
3. Caroline of Brunswick by Sir Thomas Lawrence, 1804
4. Advert for sale of properties, 1826

and almost destroyed outright by the alterations in the character of the ground.'

A plot of land belonging to Mr. Bell that lay between Royal Circus and the mill lade was purchased in 1821 by James Pedie, a Writer to the Signet (solicitor). Pedie's father had died that year and he was probably investing part of the money he had inherited. Peddie commissioned the architect, Robert Brown to lay out an overall plan for the development. Brown began as a wright (carpenter) before training as a surveyor. He then worked for Robert Reid, an established architect who planned the northern extension to Edinburgh's New Town. Brown's expertise won him a number of commissions and he was particularly noted for being able to manage the overall aspect of a development: the layout of streets, drainage and the design of the buildings. His works include the design of Melville Street and the neighbouring streets, and the Hope Park Chapel-of-Ease (now the Queen's Hall).

Pedie and Brown recognised that the site was unsuitable for the building of townhouses aimed at the better-off and as there were few shops in the nearby New Town streets, Brown devised a layout of tenements with flats aimed at the less well-off and small shops. Pedie then sold the plots to builders who sold on the completed properties or investors who contracted builders. The properties were marketed as investments, with an advert from 1826 offering an annual return from rentals of 10%.

Until 1884 St Stephen Street only ran from St Stephen's Church to Clarence Street. The rest of the street up to North West Circus was named Brunswick Street, with the exception of today's numbers 5 to 29, which were part of Baker's Place. St Stephen Place was called Market Place. Brunswick Street was named in honour of Caroline of Brunswick - Wolfenbüttel - her first name an Anglicization of the German word, Braunschweig - who married the future Prince Regent, George IV in 1795 and was a popular royal among the common people at that time. Clarence Street is named in honour of William, the Duke of Clarence and St Andrews, who became king later, in 1830. The amalgamation of Bakers Place and Brunswick Street into St Stephen Street around 1880 meant that the street numbers significantly changed, and it is not always possible to match the numbers before 1880 with those of today. Thus the place names and numbers of the relevant period are used.

The first tenement on the corner with Baker's Place (now numbers 5-13 St Stephen Street and 6-10 Baker's Place) was built for Stockbridge Mills in the 1820s by John Paton to a design by his son, David. The shops later had their fascias built out. The whole tenement was advertised for sale in 1851 and described as consisting of eight shops and three floors above, consisting of nine dwelling houses. Three of the houses have four rooms, kitchen, light closet, etc., and six have three rooms, kitchen, etc.' It sold

II. IN BRUNSWICK STREET, NEAR THE NEW MARKETS.

1. TWO DWELLING-HOUSES, first flat, No. 16, containing each three rooms and kitchen, with closets, presses, cellars, water-closets, and other conveniences. Price of each £270.

2. TWO DWELLING-HOUSES, second flat, consisting of same number of rooms and accommodations. Price of each £262, 10s.

3. TWO SHOPS on street flat, with two rooms and kitchen attached, and each with closets, cellars, &c. Price of each £330.

4. TWO SHOPS, sunk flat, with same number of rooms and accommodation. Price of each £240.

AS ALSO,

Several SMALL DWELLING-HOUSES, with Bakehouse and Oven in the sunk flat. Price of the whole £270.

The above property has been recently built; the situations are excellent and improving; and the rents will yield a handsome return.

For farther particulars apply to Mr Charles Robertson, 302, Lawnmarket; or to Robert Matthew, writer, 17, London Street.

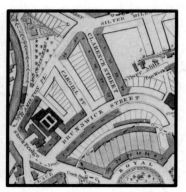

X. Also, All and Whole the several BUILDING AREAS, situated on the NORTH SIDE of BRUNSWICK STREET; and also the BUILDING AREA on the SOUTH SIDE of the said Street, immediately adjoining St. Stephen's Sessional School on the east; with Mutual Gables, Cellarage, Common Sewers, Causeway, &c., in so far as these belong to the said Sequestrated Estate.

1. Advert for sale of properties, 1829
2. Number 1 (now 97) St Stephen Street
3. Planned Cargill Street - detail from 1850 map by Robert Kirkwood (National Library of Scotland)
4. Advert for sale of land, 1846

for £3,825. Many flats had 'closets' and these were very small internal rooms – close to a cupboard but just large enough to take a narrow bed. If the small room had a window it was described as a 'light closet', while one without a window was described as a 'dark closet'.

Captain David Carnegie, who developed the Stockbridge Market, commissioned Robert Brown to design the two tenement blocks that flank the entrance and these were built around 1825. The building of Stockbridge Market is described in a later chapter.

Today's numbers 41 – 61 were built by John Cunningham between 1824 to 1829 but the land beyond to Clarence Street remained unbuilt for many years. The map from 1850 shows an intended road in the middle – named Carnegie Street. The land was released for sale as part of a sequestration in 1846. These later tenements did not follow Brown's original design concept. The tenement that adjoins the corner tenement on Clarence Street (79 -87) was completed in the 1850s and the one to its left (75 – 77) about ten years later. When the final gap was filled around 1870 (63-73) the builders added an extra storey.

Clarence Street, including the corner block with St Stephen Street, was designed by Robert Brown, except for the tenement on the other corner (29 Clarence Street / 97 St Stephen Street) that was designed by Thomas Brown. It was completed around 1835 and until around 1880 was the only house in St Stephen Street and so number 1. The history of the residents of that house and the area from it to St Stephen's Church are contained in subsequent chapters. The properties on the west side (numbers 112- 144) date from around 1885.

Robert Brown's inclusion of shops on two levels was a once common format in parts of the city. Numbers 20 to 58 were built by Andrew Wilson and George Donaldson, and 58 to 102 by Robert Gilkinson. A sale advert from 1829 provides an idea of the original format of one tenement. Above the shops were two floors, each with two flats of three rooms plus a kitchen and water closet (toilet). On the street level were two shops, each with accommodation of two rooms, kitchen and water closet. Below in the sunk area were a further two shops with one room of accommodation and two one-room flats. Separate chapters cover the histories of numbers 106, 108 and 110.

Who the first owners of properties were is not known. The properties were advertised as investment opportunities and the first Valuation Roll dated 1855 confirms that very few residents owned their property at that time. The only owner-occupiers recorded in 1855 were James Luke, who lived in Cumberland Street and owned his baker's shop and three adjoining flats that he let; three widows, one of whom also owned three other flats in her tenement; Robert Dickson who owned the pub (today The Bailie) on the corner with North West Circus Place and two shops

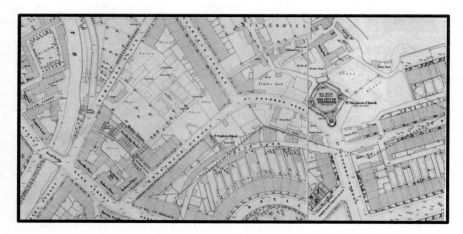

1. Rev. G. D. Cullen
2. William Balleny
3. Partly built street, 1876 Ordnance Survey map (National Library of Scotland)

11

with accommodation; and John Grant, who had a chemists shop at 24 N W Circus Place and owned his flat in Brunswick Street. All the other 190 or so flats and shops were rented.

The 1855 Valuation Rolls show that a few individuals owned a number of the properties. William Balleny was the most substantial proprietor, owing numbers 9 to 23 Brunswick Street and all 14 properties in Market Place. Balleny was Superintendent of the Edinburgh Cemetery Company. It was established in 1841 by a share issue: 'The Directors expect to open a large ornamental cemetery, conveniently situated for the inhabitants of Edinburgh. Their intention is to make the rates of burial in the new cemetery as low as possible, but also as to give a fair return to the shareholders; and also to dispose of private burying-ground at a price which will allow all classes an opportunity of now obtaining for their family a spot of ground which they can call their own.' The first of the company's cemeteries was Warriston, designed in 1842 by Edinburgh architect David Cousin. It was the first garden cemetery in Edinburgh and provided a model for several other Scottish cemeteries developed by the company.

One tenement was owned jointly by the architect, Robert Brown and Robert Winter, a flesher (butcher) who lived in one of the flats and had a shop in Jamaica Street. Other multiple owners included Reverend G. D. Cullen, Minister of South Leith who lived in Royal Terrace; Robert Robertson, a Corn Merchant who had a business in Nicholson Street and lived in Lauder Road; and Robert Smyth, a Writer to the Signet (solicitor) who lived in Hart Street. The properties on Bakers Place/Kerr Street were owned by the Stockbridge Mill Company whose mill was behind, and those in Bakers Place/Brunswick Street belonged to Andrew Tait, who owned a baker's shop in Rose Street and lived in Lynedoch Place.

George Donaldson built one of the tenements on the south side in 1826 and the various parts were advertised for sale as investment opportunities: six shops and four shops (each with one other room) were priced in blocks at £695 and £550, while the eight flats, each consisting of two rooms and a kitchen (a couple had closets) were priced individually from £126 to £156. Although the advert stated that Donaldson would show prospective buyers round, it seems unlikely that Donaldson was the owner for in the following year he was declared bankrupt. Other whole tenements continued to be marketed as an investment. In 1911 the tenement containing 25 flats (numbers 65 to 75) that had a combined income of rental of £350 in rental and feu-duty was on sale at an upset price of £2,550.

1. Washing in the kitchen sink, c.1960s
2. Poverty in Scotland, c.1950s
3. Ice cream cart, 1960s
4. The changing street - fish suppers and antiques, 1969
5. Advert for sale of properties, 1930

An uncertain future

By the 1920s St Stephen Street, India Place and other working-class streets in the area were described as being part of a 'slum district', and nothing changed over the following decades. Pat Rogan who became a city councillor in the 1950s, was a vociferous campaigner for better housing and wrote: 'One of the officials defined a slum as "Darkness, Dampness and Dilapidation". I have not heard a better description, unless one adds the word "Despair". The slums of the 'fifties and 'sixties, which had been festering from pre-war days, were truly hideous, and, in addition to the general discomfort, the families who occupied them had to contend with infestations of vermin, as well as regular outbreaks of dysentery. A pamphlet was issued by our Health Department, advising slum-dwellers how to control dysentery by the use of disinfectants, which included wiping down the toilet cistern chain after use. One bewildered woman, whose brass chain had long since gone, asked me, "How do you disinfect a piece of string?" "Burn it!" I replied.'

In 1973 45% of residents in the street lived in two-room apartments and only 60% had their own WC, while 22% shared one. Sean McNamara recounts living in a ground floor flat at number 87 from 1966 to 1973. 'There were at least two levels of basement flats below us but they were derelict all the time that I lived there - inhabited only by rats and pigeons, the windows broken, full of rubbish etc.- you didn't go down there! Our flat had two bedrooms, living room, kitchen and a toilet but there was no bathroom and I used to get washed sitting on the drainer of the kitchen sink which was at the window overlooking the back greens.'

Many residents in the 1950s and 60s did not have steady work and faced periods of unemployment. The D'Angelo family at number 5 owned an ice cream shop where the father and son worked in the summer. They also had a barrow from which they sold ice creams in Inverleith Park and elsewhere. However, in the winter they had to sign on as unemployed to get benefits, a very basic amount of money that John D'Angelo senior supplemented by busking on his violin outside the Grand Picture House.

By the 1960s there was a clear need to modernise Edinburgh and as part of the council's redevelopment plans, some streets were identified for demolition. The tenements in India Place, Saunders Street and part of Kerr Street were flattened and modern flats erected. A further threat to St Stephen Street was new guidelines that required schools to have a playing field nearby, and Stockbridge Primary School in Hamilton Place lacked one.

It is hard to imagine now, but at that time much of the New Town had ceased to be an attractive place to live for the professional class and a large number of properties were in poor condition. Thus streets such as

1. Corner of St Stephen Street, c.1910
2. Proposal for creation of new marketplace by road closure, 1973
3. St Stephen Street showing scaffolding erected for renovation
of south side properties, c.1970s

15

Cumberland Street, Fettes Row and Scotland Street, termed in the 1960s a 'tattered fringe' to the New Town, also were considered for redevelopment. Alarm at the potential loss of parts of the city's Georgian townscape to redevelopment led to the formation of the Edinburgh New Town Conservation Committee (ENTCC) in 1970.

St Stephen Street's future remained uncertain and in 1973 representatives of the Department of the Environment, Scottish Development Department, Edinburgh's Planning and Housing departments and ENTCC met with local people and compiled a report on its possible future. That research found that half the residents had lived in the street for 21 years, tended to be elderly and 40% were owner occupiers. The report was ambivalent about preserving some parts of the street. The north side, with Stockbridge Market long gone, was not considered to have significant architectural merit, nor was the upper part of St Stephen Street (apart from the two churches). The tenement on the corner with Clarence Street had a large vertical crack through the building and was scheduled for demolition, next to it was the unattractive 1900 building that was operating as a relatively run-down music venue, and on the opposite side undistinguished 1885 properties.

However, the south side was seen to have architectural merit and a strong case was made for it to be preserved even if the other parts were demolished: 'If costs should prove hopelessly beyond the city's means and the area in part written off, the south side of St Stephen Street must be retained. It would then read continuously with the Royal Circus and North West Circus Place. With the bowed block at the west end and St Stephen's School at the east end it would still form a well-balanced architectural unit. It would become the northern frontier of the New Town.'

The report highlighted that fact that due to the poor condition of properties would-be entrepreneurs, mainly young, had taken advantage of the street's low rents and the shops now housed a fashionable diversity of traders: of the 28 shops, only two were vacant. One idea was to close the street off from traffic between St Stephen's School/Clarence Street and Kerr Street, form a new market area where Stockbridge Market had been and thus create a stylish open marketplace, Although that never transpired neither did the possible demolition of the north side and the highlighted architectural significance of the south side led to a programme of refurbishment and refacing of numbers 20 – 58 in the late 1970s, and major structural repairs saved number 97. Also in the late 1970s properties on the north side received grants from the recently created Edinburgh New Town Conservation Committee to help renovate their properties. Thus, the only demolition that occurred was in 1991 when the large building next to St Stephen's Church, then a music club, burnt down and was replaced with a modern block of flats.

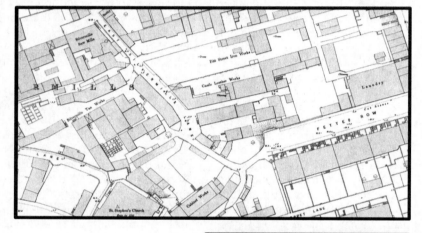

1. The mill lade at Damside, 1858
(photo - Thomas Begbie)
2. View of workshops and factories in
Silvermills, c. 1900
3. Silvermills - detail from 1894
Ordnance Survey map (National
Library of Scotland)
4. Original painted street number on
property in St Stephen Street

Life in the street

The land that James Pedie bought on which to develop Brunswick Street was not an ideal site for housing. It adjoined the mill lade that had been built to draw water from the Water of Leith to power mills and other workspaces to the east of Pedie's land at Silvermills; many of which exuded harmful chemicals and odours. Also, by the early 1800s, some, such as the Stockbridge Mill, had introduced steam engines with resulting noise and smoke. In 1888 it was reported: 'Many of these industries, being of great antiquity, are carried on on old lines. It is not to be wondered at, therefore, that they are often complained of by the inhabitants in St Stephen Street and Clarence Street.' Also, the land's proximity to the Water of Leith and being at the bottom of the hill, meant it was prone to flooding and the street's sunk areas suffered from dampness.

The rented flats became home to a diversity of the working class as the occupations of residents show: flesher (butcher), silk dyer, tailor, wright, shop assistant, lady's nurse, porter, mason, dairyman, shoemaker, music teacher, midwife, lace cleaner, coalman, fishing rod maker, toy merchant, cook, seamstress, joiner, blacksmith, staymaker (corsets), cabman, rope maker, labourer and house painter. Many families were large and overcrowding was common. Charles Stewart, a tailor, rented two rooms in the street in the 1850s and this was home to him, his wife and four children, all aged under ten, as well as being his workspace. Some flats were subdivided and others operated as lodging houses, often with two or three lodgers per room.

As almost all were rented, it is unlikely that many properties were well maintained by the absent landlords and deficiencies would have been exacerbated by the steady turnover of tenants, not all of whom would have been house-proud. The street was badly lit: 'St Stephen Street is the worst lighted street in the city, and the most dangerous for the ordinary public at night, to say nothing of those who stagger about three sheets to the wind, and are often seen to disappear head foremost down some of the death-traps which abound in this street – I refer to the sunk areas.'

For the majority of residents in the 19th century religion would have been a significant part of their lives. The normally bustling street would have had quite a different feel on a Sabbath morning with all the shops and workshops closed, and families, dressed in the best clothes they could afford, setting off for church. While any Jews would have observed the Sabbath the day before and attended the Jewish Synagogue in Richmond Court, and Roman Catholics would have attended St Mary's in Broughton Street, the susceptibility for Scottish Protestant worshippers in the 19th century to split over doctrinal differences meant they could be headed in a variety of directions. The Church Section of the 1865 Post Office

18

SCOTCH WASHING

W. K. MUNRO   EDINBURGH

1. Dressmaker (PBS series *The Victorian Slum House*)
2. Chimney Sweep, c.1910
3. Blacksmith, c.1900s
4. Scotch Washing, 'a method of washing clothes to be seen by the river' - carte-de-visite by W. Munro, c.1870s

Directory listed the Church of Scotland, The Free Church of Scotland, United Presbyterians, Scottish Episcopalians, English Episcopalians, Baptists, Wesleyan Methodists, Congregationalists, United Methodist Free Church, The Primitive Methodists, Synod of Original Seceders, Reformed Presbyterian Church, Quakers and Glassites

The strong Presbyterian faction against any non-religious activity on a Sunday led to ludicrous claims such as that God's vengeance at trains travelling on Sundays had been responsible for the Tay Bridge collapse in which 75 people died. Thomas Talon, the minister of St Vincent's Chapel was so infuriated by such an idea that he published his sermon mocking the idea: 'Do these men believe the Ruler of the Universe was waiting at the Tay Bridge to destroy the poor railway travellers?'

Ill-health, high child mortality and limited life span was common. In the 1823 cholera outbreak Brunswick Street was one of a small number of Edinburgh streets listed as having cases. Another scourge was smallpox; while The Vaccination Act of 1853 made vaccination compulsory for all infants in the first three months of life, and made defaulting parents liable to a fine or imprisonment, some resisted. In 1874 Andrew Howieson of Brunswick Street refused and in court pleaded guilty but said he had contravened the law for conscience sake. He appeared in court over the following two years for the same offence and eventually agreed to have his child vaccinated to avoid imprisonment. The city's public-health return in 1915 showed that the death rate in St Stephen's ward was the highest in the city and in 1932 infant mortality in the area was 182 to 1,000, also the highest in the city.

By 1888 the mill lade had become an open sewer: 'The lade is now the receptacle of all kinds of refuse, is highly charged with organic matter and gives rise to objectionable odours.' It was unfenced and in 1853 'while some boys were amusing themselves on the edge of the mill-lade, in the rear of 35 Brunswick Street, James Laidlaw, the two-and-a-half years old son of the baker in India Place, fell into the water and drowned.' Some years later, John Dunlop, of whom more later, saved a young child from a similar fate. It was not until 1895 that the by-then unused lade was fenced off and eventually covered over.

Many struggled financially, particularly large families. In the early 1860s St Stephen's Church provided free coal and other support during the winter to 230 local families and ran a soup kitchen all year that fed more than 100 families. It is no surprise that the longest established shop in the street from 1860 through to the 1950s was a pawnbroker. Understandably, crime was common, although the great majority who lived in the street worked hard, and led honest lives, in spite of deprivation.

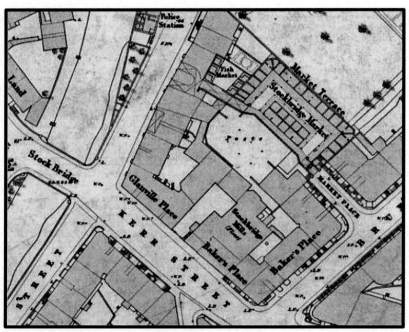

1. Site of Stockbridge Mills - detail from 1851 map by Robert Kirkwood (National Library of Scotland)
2. A flour mill, 1920

21

Stockbridge Mills

Stockbridge Mills was built on the south-east side of the bridge (behind today's Baker's Place) around 1760 and by 1800 was owned by Alexander Kedslie, who lived next to the mills. Around 1815 he installed a steam engine, as the mill required more power for grinding the corn than could be supplied by the mill lade. The locals complained: 'The machine is a nuisance and destroys the comforts and enjoyments of local people, the air being so tainted with smoke from the engine.' One of the leading protesters was the painter, Henry Raeburn and eventually the issue ended up in court with some of the city's leading lawyers involved. Kedslie's defence team included Francis Jeffrey, later Lord Advocate.

Raeburn's lawyer stated: 'So vast a column of smoke comes from this engine, that clothes hung out to dry are made as black as before they were washed. My clients are deprived of the use of their gardens, hot-houses, &c. and the value of their properties are thereby reduced.' Francis Jeffrey responded: 'Is the injury so much as to warrant the putting down of the machine? In the suburbs of all large and populous cities, disagreeable manufactories of all kinds must exist; and while the nice and elegant part of the community might find it necessary to remove all impolite trades and employments from their vicinity, yet the increase of luxuries required also an increase of manufactures and machinery of all kinds.' The jury sided with Kedslie: 'The engine is useful, and not offensive.'

The dispute may have led to Kedslie's bankruptcy the following year, and ownership of the mills passed to the Incorporation of Bakers. A few years later Kedslie sold his adjoining house and grounds and Stockbridge Market was built on the site.

By 1849 William Hay & Son had taken over the mill and in that year the premises caught fire. Military personnel from the castle joined the fire brigade in fighting the blaze and although grain and machinery were destroyed, the mill soon was back in action. The business was then leased to Alexander and Robert Tod at £400 per annum: 'The mills contain nine pairs of Stone; and grind about 800 quarters of wheat weekly (a quarter was two stone). The superior quality of the flour is well known in the market. There is a good fall and constant supply of water, by which a portion of the machinery is driven and there is a powerful steam-engine for driving the remainder of the machinery. There are extensive granaries of five storeys high attached to a five-stalled stable and a counting-room. These are all enclosed by one gate.'

The Tod brothers later purchased the mill and A & R Tod Ltd, also opened a large mill in Leith. The Stockbridge Mills closed in 1921.

1. & 2. Fire
brigade dealing
with the
aftermath of the
mills' explosion,
1901

The Great Explosion

In July 1901 there was a massive explosion at the mill; six people were killed and many more injured. 'A gas engine, which had been used for supplying auxiliary power, was in course of removal, having been replaced by electric motors. This work was being done by engineers from an outside firm, and it is supposed that when using a naked light they had uncoupled the connection without turning off the gas, thus causing the explosion. The force of it in the confined space caused the wall between the mill and Mr. Bowie's shop to be blown out into the shop; practically the entire contents of the shop were blown into the street and the street was strewn with sugar, tins of beef and other groceries. A shop-man across the street had a somewhat narrow escape, being missed by a tin of meat projected into the shop. The wall between Mr. Robert Bowie's shop and that of Mr. Brock, hatter and hosier, the next shop down the street, was blown through, and Mr. Brock and a customer were fortunate in escaping without hurt. Bowie's shop was set on fire, but the flames did not get hold before they were rapidly subdued by the detachment of the fire brigade from the neighbouring station.

'Meantime the staff of clerks in the offices above the shops had a sad fright, the office heaving as if earthquake had occurred. They rushed for the street, but had the presence of mind to carry with them books and documents. The mill premises got fairly ablaze in an alarming fashion, and it was soon apparent that a considerable portion of the mill containing valuable machinery was lost. Several of the men escaped by throwing themselves down the bag shoot, while one or two others jumped down the stairs.'

Six men died, including the mill's manager and three of the workmen who had been removing the gas engine, Later, transpired that the Workmen's Compensation Act, which was designed to secure a reasonable provision for the dependants of workmen who were fatally injured at work, did not cover this disaster. So John Smith, a mill owner in Leith wrote to The Scotsman: 'Sir, Now that the public inquiry into the circumstances of this disaster has taken place might I suggest that some steps should be taken by public subscription to make provision for the widows and children of the workmen who met their death in so sad a manner. There are five widows each with a family of young children, nearly all of whom are in destitute circumstances and I would suggest that a public subscription should be started, and a committee appointed while the circumstances of the ease are fresh in the public mind.' His suggestion was taken up and the Lord Provost chaired the committee that raised money for the support of the deceased men's families.

1. St Stephen's Church by Thomas Hosmer, engraved by E. Stalker, 1829
2. Original interior of St Stephen's Church

25

St Stephen's Church

Originally, it was proposed that the church be built in India Street and called St Vincent's but the present site and the name, St Stephen's, were finally chosen. The steeply sloping site was problematic and not all were convinced that the architect, William Henry Playfair, successfully overcame the difficulties. For many years ministers suffered from poor acoustics and the clock that is reputed to have the longest pendulum in Europe often went wrong.

The imposing building opened in 1828 with Rev Dr William Muir as its first minister and drew its congregation from the well-off professionals. In its early days its elders were reputed to be 'a group of the wealthiest men in Edinburgh'.

In the 19th century sermons lasted from 50 to 60 minutes so no doubt parents had to take a plentiful supply of sucking sweets to ensure their children endured these in peace; one being Robert Louis Stevenson, whose family worshipped there. Like a number of churches in the city, it was not until 1880 that the church decided to allow instrumental music at services and commissioned an organ at a cost of £1,300.

While St Stephen's drew its congregation from the wealthier parts of the New Town, it did not turn its back on Brunswick Street and other disadvantaged areas nearby. The congregation established a Sabbath School that provided some education for poor children and then built St Stephen's School. The congregation also paid for donations of free coal and provided a soup kitchen to help local needy families. Throughout most of the 19th century ladies in the congregation ran 'a work society that affords employment to upwards of seventy females from the parish.' There local women made a variety of clothes: 'of the best materials and sold at very low prices; articles may be obtained any day by applying to the Teacher of the Infant School.' For many years the congregation made the largest annual contribution to foreign missions of any in the city and, in 1842, funded its own foreign mission in India at Ghospara on the banks of the Hoogly, which included a school.

Lord Sands writing in 1928 about the church's centenary relates that the first wedding held in St Stephen's took place in 1881; probably the marriage of Hugh Nicholson of Spittal Hall, Cheshire to Margaret Gifford, the only daughter of William Broadfoot. Lord Sands explained why so few weddings took place in church in the 18th century: 'That marriage should be celebrated in church is prescribed in the Directory for Public Worship. But the rule was long totally, and is still very generally, disregarded in Scotland. This arose probably because marriage in the house or the manse was found to be more convenient, and the Puritan idea, which long prevailed, forbade the attachment of any special sanctity to the

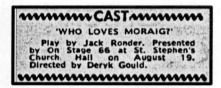

1. Rev. Dr William Muir
2. Rev. Lauchlan MacLean Watt
3. Marriage of Kenneth Little and Ada Heggie in St Stephen's Church, 1939
4. Advert for On Stage's Fringe production of *Who Loves Moraig?*, 1967
5. Poster for Aurora Nova's Fringe season, 2001

House of Worship. So the celebration of marriage either at the bride's house or at the manse came to be firmly established by custom. The celebration of marriage in Presbyterian churches was resumed only within living memory.'

In 1887 a programme of improvements was carried out: 'The seating of the building has hitherto been somewhat uncomfortable, but now the pews have been covered and refurbished; a handsome pulpit and choir circle of walnut have been constructed; the walls have been repainted and decorated, the prevailing tint being chrome yellow relieved here and there with pretty medallions, representations of flowers and fruit; and the dome has been glazed; and from the centre, a fine gasalier (gas-powered chandelier) has been suspended.' The acoustics also were improved. In 1911 Dr Lauchlan McLean Watt became the church's minister and served until 1923. He was a prolific author in prose and verse, and a bagpipe player. His time as a chaplain with the Gordon Highlanders during the First World War is described in that chapter. Although St Stephen Street has never been visited by a Royal, in 1922 Dr Watt was invited to delivered the sermon at a service at Crathie Church attended by King George V and members of the Royal family: 'The Rev. Lauchlan MacLean Watt of St Stephen's, Edinburgh, taking for his text "Come unto Me, and I will give you rest," preached an eloquent sermon.'

By the 1950s the congregation had declined and the building was remodelled: the gallery level was floored over to become the church space, with a large hall created below. The hall has hosted many events, including Fringe performances. One of the first companies to use the venue was On Stage 66, who performed there in 1967. In 2001 Wolfgang Hoffmann, a dancer, director and producer from former East Germany, opened the venue as Aurora Nova, named after the Russian battleship that fired the first shot in the October Revolution. For seven years the venue brought some of the finest physical theatre in the world to Edinburgh. 'This festival-within-a-festival is a must for those seeking out the most adventurous Fringe programming.'

In 1992 the building became a community centre and in the early 21st century its bell was silenced after it was found to exceed night-time noise limits. The building was bought in 2017 by Peter Schaufuss, sometime Artistic Director of the English National Ballet, who said that he planned to make the main hall 'a world-class theatre, one that will attract productions from leading companies from around the world.'

1. Interior of St Vincent's Chapel
2. Detail of stained glass window adapted from Robert Scott Lauder's painting, *Christ Teachest Humility.* Lauder was born in Silvermills in 1803
3. Commandery of Lochore Emergency Ambulance Corps, 1970s
4. Poster for Festival of the Sacred Arts, 2018

St Vincent's Chapel

Scotland has a long tradition of religious dissent and in the mid-19th century factional splits led to a flurry of new church building. In 1842 the Reverend David Drummond, a curate at Holy Trinity, Dean Bridge, seceded from the Scottish Episcopal Church, as he rejected the authority of the Scottish bishops, and built a chapel in Rutland Place. He appointed Rev. Richard Hibbs, an Evangelical English clergyman, curate but in 1854 another schism occurred and Hibbs left to found St Vincent's.

The chapel was designed by the Hay brothers in the 14th century Decorated Gothic style favoured by Catholic-minded Anglicans and Episcopalians. Opened as Christ's English Episcopal Chapel in 1857, it soon was renamed the St Vincent's Chapel. Hibbs left for England after just two years and was replaced by Thomas Talon, an Irishman who had served as a priest in England. A leading member of the congregation, William Forbes Skene, the great historian and Historiographer Royal for Scotland, bought St Vincent's in 1875 as a memorial to his descendants and later gifted it to the congregation..

Anne Clutterbuck recalls attending in the 1930s: 'I went to matins mostly – all the services were simple and quiet but we usually had good organ music. Most of the congregation came from Stockbridge and were elderly. I used to leave the baby in her pram in the passage and the elderly verger would let me know immediately if she woke.' In 1971 the building was sold to Lt Col. Robert Gayre; the interior was altered and heraldic stained glass by A. Carrick Whalen added. In 1987 the use of the building passed to the Trustees of the Commandery of Lochore of the Military and Hospitaller Order of St Lazarus of Jerusalem – a Christian ecumenical fraternal order constituted in 1910 by French Catholics - as its private chapel, although it continued to be used for Episcopalian services.

In 1949, in response to concern at a potential nuclear attack, the government established The Civil Defence Corps, a civilian volunteer organisation that would supposedly take control of its local area in a major national emergency. By March 1956 it had 330,000 personnel across the UK. When the Corp was abolished in 1968 the Commandery of Lochore established a small volunteer emergency ambulance corps. It was planned that the headquarters of the corps would be at St Vincent's Chapel's hall but this did not happen; instead Glasgow became the headquarters. By the early 1970s the ambulance corps had seven ambulances in operation based in Glasgow, Edinburgh, Galashiels, Stirling and Ayr. The Corps was disbanded in the 1990s. In 2020 the Commandery was dissolved and passed the church back to the chapel's Vestry. The venue has been used for a range of events, mostly music; from sacred music to rousing pop.

The MEETING HOUSE for the DEAF and DUMB in BRUNSWICK STREET is OPEN for DIVINE WORSHIP EVERY SUNDAY FORENOON and AFTERNOON at the Usual Hours. The Services are in the Manual Alphabet, and by Signs. Members of the various Protestant Denominations attend Sacrament at their own Churches. Those who do not belong to any particular Denomination are provided for by the Missionary.

ALEX. BLACKWOOD, Missionary.
DAVID LAIRD, Secretary.

1. Advert, 1865
2. The Deaf Church in 49/51 Albany Street
3. Alexander Blackwood
4. Signed Church Service

Deaf & Dumb Church

In 1760 the Edinburgh Deaf and Dumb Institution, the world's first regular school for Deaf and Dumb children, was established by Thomas Braidwood in Edinburgh at St Leonard's Hill in what is now Dumbiedykes Road (named after the deaf scholars who were seen signing away along the then unnamed road). In 1830 the first Deaf-led church services were initiated by an Edinburgh group of Deaf adults who wished to meet for prayers and social contact, and in 1835 Alexander Blackwood, who had been a day pupil at the Edinburgh Deaf and Dumb Institution, established the Edinburgh Deaf and Dumb Benevolent Society, the first of its kind.

By the 1860s the signed Deaf-led church services were held in St Stephen's School and between 30 and 50 men and women of all ages attended the morning and afternoon services that were led by Blackwood. In 1864 Blackwood was told the congregation would have to attend the normal services at St James's Episcopal Chapel. A Deaf and Dumb member wrote to the newspaper complaining: 'At a normal church service all we perceive is a human in the pulpit opening and shutting his mouth, and an assembly of people sitting with due reverence and seeming to like it. This at first may encourage an undefinable awe, and perhaps a sort of bastard religious feeling, but it soon wears off, and we are compelled to sit Sunday after Sunday in mere vacancy. Books of all kinds are beyond the average comprehension of most; and the Liturgy of the Scottish Episcopal Church more so.'

Fortunately, the signed services at St Stephen's School were reinstated. In 1867 'a soiree for the deaf and dumb residing in Edinburgh' was held in the school. 'It is believed to have been the fullest gathering of the kind that ever took place in Edinburgh. Also present were a good number of hearing friends. After tea, the chairman delivered a suitable address in the manual language, and several other addresses were delivered by deaf and dumb gentlemen, which were fully applauded. Mr. Blackwood acted as interpreter for the benefit of those present who did understand the manual language. Afterwards the meeting adjourned to a separate hall where a series of very interesting magic lantern views were exhibited.'

In 1889 the Society bought Number 49 Albany Street and re -vamped the interior, including creating a church at the rear specifically designed to meet the visual needs of its congregation, with pews facing the pulpit and no central aisle.

THE EARLY HISTORY

or

THE GOSPEL

or

THE KINGDOM OF GOD

IN BRITAIN

WITH

HISTORICAL, CRITICAL, AND SOCIAL REMINISCENCES

or

PERSONS, PLACES, AND EVENTS

COMPILED BY WILLIAM NORRIE

VOLUME I.

1. Robert Roberts
2. Church of Scotland Reward Stamp engraved by Gilbert Oliver
3. Advert for lecture by John Norrie, 1889
4. Advert for Norrie & Co., 1885
5. *Early History of the Kingdom of God in Britain* by William Norrie, 1904. In his introduction he wrote: 'Only ten copies have been produced. The impression has been made thus limited, because those interested in such a narrative are a little flock and the number of those whose interest takes the form of approval is believed to be much less.'

The Norrie Family

Robert and Isabella Norrie, who lived and ran a grocer's shop at number 24, were Baptists. They had four children and the eldest, Isabella, married Gilbert Oliver, an engraver, in 1860. In 1863 Gilbert established his own engraving firm that grew to employ nine staff. He engraved and published a series of sets of attractive Reward Stamps on behalf of the Church of Scotland between the years 1890 and 1913. These were issued to children attending Sunday School as attendance rewards or for good behaviour.

Jane - described as 'serious and devout'- married eighteen-year-old Robert Roberts who was working as a reporter on The Caledonian Mercury. As Jane sang in the Baptist church choir and Robert's mother was a strongly religious Calvinistic Baptist, it is likely they met through the church, although Robert was an early convert to the Christadelphians, a religious group established by an American, John Thomas. Robert and Jane settled in Birmingham where he was employed as a reporter although much of his time was taken up proselytising, and he became the de facto leader of the Christadelphian community in Britain. In 1898 Jane accompanied him on a preaching tour of Australia and New Zealand. On the return journey, Robert died in San Francisco. He is buried in New York beside John Thomas. Jane died in 1919.

William, who worked as a Lithographer Printer, possibly in Gilbert's firm, also became a convert to the Christadelphian faith. As did his younger brother, John who ran a bookshop for many years until 1879 when, in an unusual change of career, he became a chiropodist. In 1885, however, he split from the Christadelphians and became President of the Edinburgh branch of the Conditional Immortality Mission.

Two of John's sons died young. David joined his father in promoting the Conditional Immortality Mission and while in Huddersfield in 1911 lecturing on 'The state of the blessed dead' dropped dead on returning to his lodgings that evening. He was just 35. The eldest son, John had a dazzling academic career. After Edinburgh University he sat the extremely competitive examinations for the Indian Civil Service and came top in Britain. This earned him the Boden Sanskrit Scholarship at Balliol College, Oxford. He then joined the India Civil Service and was posted to Oudh in 1897 but died of cholera within a year, aged just 25. The third son, Gilbert, worked with his father as a chiropodist and lived into his sixties. What his religious preference was is not known.

1. 2. & 3. Images of working-class Victorians – fireman, butcher & midwife
4. Advert by James Main, 1828
5. Marriage announcement, 1858

Residents of 27 Brunswick Street / 45 St Stephen Street

This and the following three chapters describe a number of people who lived in this tenement to provide a partial portrait of the residents of the street in its first 100 years.

James Main lived in one of the flats from 1831 to 1835. He had opened a bookshop in George Street in 1828: 'James Main, Bookseller & Stationer, has on sale a large proportion of old and curious tracts and publications rarely to be met with, and at such prices must prove an inducement to collectors.' He moved to live in Howe Street and a few years later his shop was gone.

James Luke, who features in a following chapter, recently had married Catherine Rankin and they set up home here; she bore five children in the house. As there was a high infant mortality rate, most couples had large families and for fertile women, motherhood could absorb almost all reserves of physical and emotional energy for at least a decade. Pregnancy at this time was a period of considerable vulnerability, especially for those living in crowded accommodation as most births took place in the home. Thus a midwife such as Mrs Cameron, who bought one of the flats in 1835 and lived there for many years, would have been a significant figure in the neighbourhood. She was a widow and lived with her unmarried daughter, who worked as a dressmaker. Those too poor to afford a midwife could seek help from the Edinburgh Lying-In Institution that had been established in 1824 to assist with the births of 'poor married women at their own house' and offered 'every requisite attendance, either by a Medical Gentleman or a Midwife, to poor married women; to furnish them with the necessary medicines; to supply the most needy of them with the temporary use of Bed Linen, Flannels, Blankets, etc., and with any other addition to the means of comfort and health that may be essentially necessary.'

Although Mrs Lyon, a widow in her fifties, who rented her four-room flat plus kitchen, had three unmarried children living with her - Allison (25) and Catherine (20), both dressmakers, and Walter (15), a music seller's apprentice - she also took in lodgers. At the 1841 census she had four: John Graham (25) a teacher, William Black (30) a furnishing shop keeper, John Jameson (40) a cabinetmaker and Rev. James Marshall (40) a minister. To make ends meet many residents took in lodgers, and two or even three might share one room. Unusually, the Rev Marshall lodged with Mrs Lyon for almost twenty years.

In June 1858 Janet, the eldest daughter of Mr and Mrs Russell, married Thomas Thomson in the house, with the Rev. Gray of Lady Yester's Church attending. In the 19th century almost all wedding ceremonies took place in the house of the bride or groom, usually in the morning. These

Mysterious Case of Suicide by a Young Lady in Stockbridge

At an early hour yesterday morning; the inhabitants of Stockbridge were thrown into the greatest excitement by the announcement that a young lady had committed suicide at Number 27 Brunswick Street. The deceased, a female between 20 and 25 years of age, named Martha Moffat, arrived from London by steamer on Monday afternoon, accompanied by a man about 60 years of age, who goes by the name of Gray. They engaged two bed rooms and two sitting rooms in a house on the second floor, occupied by Mr Russell, the woman representing her companion as her uncle. On Tuesday the strangers were out in company the greater part of the day, and in the evening they had toddy together. On Wednesday morning the woman asked Mr Russell to direct her to a medical man, as she was afraid her companion had drugged her toddy the previous evening. Her wish was complied with, and she expressed to the doctor considerable distrust of Mr Gray, alleging that he had brought her away from London to get rid of her, and would not furnish her with the means of returning, as she earnestly desired to do. The doctor prescribed for her, judging her case to be one of morbid nervous excitement. She went to bed that night between ten and eleven o'clock, leaving Mr Gray at his toddy in the parlour adjoining her bed-room. Mrs Russell went to her room about ten minutes past eleven, and found her apparently asleep. About five o'clock on Thursday morning Mr and Mrs Russell were aroused by Mr Gray knocking at their bed-room door. He wished Mrs Russell to come to Mrs Gray (both parties are confident he said Mrs Gray) as he thought she was worse; indeed he feared she was dead. Mrs Russell proceeded to the bed-room, and was struck with horror on reaching the threshold to see its inmate stretched on her back on the floor with her throat cut in the most frightful manner. The body was quite cold, and had evidently been dead for some hours. The police were instantly sent for, and the body conveyed to the Police Office. Mr Gray was taken into custody, and the whole circumstances of the case were yesterday investigated at great length by the Procurator-Fiscal.

Article from Caledonian Mercury, 3 September 1858

were simple ceremonies, with a minister attending to give a blessing, and were only attended by close family, but followed by a wedding breakfast elsewhere to which friends were invited.

It was not uncommon for those who rented rooms, as Mr and Mrs Russell did, to have to deal with the death of a lodger as many were elderly. However, the death that took place in their flat three months after their daughter's wedding was unusually upsetting as the Caledonian Mercury reported (see opposite). Later, it was reported that the dead woman's father explained that she suffered from fits of depression and on past occasions had 'stated that she felt a strong inclination to open the window and jump out of it.' Thus, it was resolved that Miss Moffat had taken her own life, although some thought the manner in which she had committed suicide questionable, and there was the ambiguous nature of the relationship between Miss Moffat and her 'uncle', Mr Gray.

At the 1861 census the eight flats contained twenty-eight adults, two children and one infant. The men's occupations included engineer, baker, butcher, law clerk and cabinetmaker. Three of the women worked as dressmakers, and others as a laundress, a janitor and a wool store keeper. From 1862 Thomas Monteith, who ran the wine and spirits merchant at number 1 (now The Bailie), lived in the house for a year or so.

John Dewar, a bank messenger in his late 50s bought Mrs Lyon's flat in the mid-1860s and lived there with his wife. Following her death he was looked after by his unmarried daughter until his death around 1881. At the 1871 census, the occupations of the other male occupants were cabinetmaker (three), tailor cutter, butler, plumber (two), joiner and the manager of the Co-operative store that had opened in the street.

In 1884 the tenement was renamed and renumbered 45 St Stephen Street. At that time William and Lilias Ramsay were living with their three teenage children and a baby in a two-room house in the sunk basement. They were in their late thirties and both had been married before. As divorce was uncommon, it is likely their first spouses had died. William had two sons from his first marriage, both of whom were working at Waddie & Co along the street: William (17) as an apprentice print machine attendant and John (15) as an apprentice compositor. Lilias had a daughter, Helen (15) who was still at school, and they had a shared new baby. William was a cabman as was his father who lived at Stephen Place. William, senior had given a testimonial for Doan's Backache Kidney Pills that appeared in many newspapers: 'I have been a cab-driver in this city for 38 years, ever since the first Queen's Review, and of course I have been exposed to all sorts of weather. I have frequently caught severe colds, and they all seemed to settle in my back, just over my kidneys. These pains were very severe, and at times I have been so bad I could hardly raise myself from my bed. I had rheumatism in my shoulders and knees, and the

1. A horse-drawn van delivery in Edinburgh, 1910
2. Laundresses, c.1900
3. Compositor, c.1930
4. Advert, 1910
5. Boy taking clothes to pawnshop, c.1900

pain has often been unbearable. This was the state of my health when I heard about Doan's Pills, and as they were recommended for bad backs I decided to give them a trial. I must say they did me a wonderful deal of good. I have been much freer from pain since taking them, and I shall continue with the pills for I am sure they will eventually cure me." Signed William Ramsey. Doan's Backache Kidney Pills are sold by all chemists and drug stores at 2s 9d per box (six boxes 13s9d.' Perhaps in exchange for his testimonial, William received a free supply of pills and shared them with his son.

As everyone in the tenement lived in close proximity, problematic neighbours were an annoyance. In 1890 the other tenants at number 27 were forced to call the authorities about William Wilson, a dairyman who lived in the sunk area. He ended up in court charged that: 'on various dates he had accumulated within the house occupied by him a quantity of filth and other offensive matter. In the course of the evidence it transpired that when the inspectors visited the house they found it in an extremely filthy condition. Several pails of ashes, old bread, potato peelings and other rubbish were lying in the lobby.'

The 1901 census records that the occupants of the larger flats were a house painter, his wife and three children, plus a lodger; a widow with four working children, plus two lodgers; a baker, his wife and three children; an unmarried woman in her late fifties who worked in a china dealers shop and had three lodgers; a van driver, George Baillie, his wife and four children; a family of six, plus one lodger; and a family of seven. The two small flats in the sunk area were lived in by a widow and her two children, and a married couple with no children.

The van driver, George Baillie, worked for a cabinetmaker's firm and clearly was not a man to be trifled with. In 1900 the horse pulling the van suddenly came to a halt in Pitt Street. As George and his two work mates were trying to encourage the horse to move, a man who owned a laundry in the street rushed out and began accusing them of ill-treating the horse. The fracas led to the three suing the laundryman for slander. In court they also claimed he had brandished a knife. They won their case and George was awarded £23 in damages. Perhaps it was no coincidence that George bred terrier dogs. He exhibited these at Edinburgh's dog shows and advertised dogs for sale: 'Yorkshire terrier, "Northern Wonder", rich, golden tan and blue coat, the sire of Kirk Billy, champion in the Edinburgh Kennel Club Show.'

At the last available census in 1911 there were 38 adults and 10 children living in the eight flats. Occupations included baker, plumber, footman, charwoman, clerk, barman, tramcar worker and three brothers who all worked at Waddie & Co. By the early 1960s seven of the flats were owned by the City of Edinburgh.

1. Advert for The Canada West Land Agency, 1883
2. Report into the quality of Edinburgh bread, 1857
3. Photo dated 1859 of group at Oxford, containing George Rankine Luke. 1st Viscount
Bryce, Albert Venn Dicey, Thomas Hill Green, Sir Thomas Erskine Holland, John
Warneford Hoole, Aeneas James George MacKay, John Nichol, Joseph Frank Payne and
Algernon Charles Swinburne.

The Luke family

James Luke, who was born in 1803, was apprenticed as a baker and by 1828 was working in Edinburgh. He married Catherine Rankin that year and they set up home at number 27, next door to their baker's shop at number 25: probably a ground floor shop with an oven in the basement.

Six children were born in the house: James (1829), Mary (1831), Margaret (1832), Isabella (1834), George (1836) and John (1838). In 1841 the census records that, unusually for Brunswick Street residents, the Lukes employed two young sisters as servants.

Tragedy struck the family as Catherine died in 1845, aged just 36, leaving James to bring up his young children. The family's grief was compounded the following year by the death of Isabella. While it is likely that all the children attended St Stephen's School when young, the three oldest children began working in the bakery in their early teens.

The exception was George. He was recognised as particularly gifted and his father paid for him to attend the Edinburgh Academy in Hamilton Place. He was a pupil there from 1847 to 1853 and won numerous prizes, culminating with becoming the school's 'dux' in his final year. George then studied at the University of Glasgow and was awarded a scholarship to study at Balliol College, Oxford. There he also won many awards, including a prize for his essay, *Nikais: A Greek Dialogue On Superstition,* which was published in 1858. At Oxford he became a close friend of Algernon Charles Swinburne, later a renowned poet, playwright, novelist, and critic. Sadly, tragedy struck the Luke family for the third time as George's bright future was cut short in March 1862 as he drowned in the Isis River in Oxford when his row-boat overturned.

In the 1850s James and his family moved to a flat he purchased at 72 Cumberland Street. He continued to own the baker's shop and the flat at number 27 that he let. Mary married John Paris, a young architect in 1862 but Margaret, James and John remained unmarried and worked in the bakery. By 1879 only James, junior was still alive and he sold the bakery and began a new career as a land and emigration agent with the Canada West Land Agency.

1. Advert, 1862
2. Alison Dunlop
3. A Victorian Cabinetmaker's workshop
4. Scottish Rugby Team, 1871

The Dunlop family

When Charles Dunlop married Jessie Mercer in 1833 they set up home in a rented flat at number 27. He had a cabinet-making business that later operated from a workshop on ground near St Stephen's Church. They had three children: John Charles (1834), Alison Hay (1836) and James Mercer (1837).

Charles was a member of the congregation of St Stephen's Church and like others in the church wanted to ensure that local children received an education. As at that time there was no free school in the area, Charles and others established a Local Sabbath School that gave working class children lessons on Sundays in private houses rented for the purpose. In Charles's class the school furniture consisted of three forms made by him, which were carried into the room on Saturday night, taken out on Monday morning and stowed away during the week.

In 1836 the church built St Stephens School and the three Dunlop children would have been educated there, although it is likely that they had additional schooling as all three became keen antiquarians, and Alison - and possibly her brothers - could read and converse freely in several foreign languages.

James studied divinity and became a minister in the United Presbyterian church. His ministries included Biggar and Pollokshaws, Glasgow. In 1876 he married his cousin, Jessie Mercer, whose family lived in Tasmania, and the wedding was held at number 27. He became ill from pleurisy in his early sixties and was forced to retire from the ministry. He died at his house in Ferry Road in 1900.

Alison began working as a governess but as the family business grew, joined the firm to manage the administration. She remained unmarried, although in 1863 she became friendly with a young minister and poet, Thomas Davidson. As he travelled widely for the church and later became an invalid, living in Jedburgh, the two barely met but exchanged weekly letters until his death in 1870. Alison loved to write and thanks to a scheme established by The Edinburgh Ladies' Educational Association to provide higher education for women, attended classes and won first prize for English Literature. She also was an early city conservationist and at a time when many ancient buildings in the Old Town were being demolished, rummaged among the debris, saving distinctive fragments. She also began researching and recording vignettes of Edinburgh's past life, a number of which were published in The Scotsman newspaper.

John joined, and later ran, his father's firm and expanded into new areas, becoming a house factor, estate agent, undertaker and antique dealer. While his brother enjoyed fishing, John was keener on ball games and being on the committee of the Grange Cricket Club, was involved in the

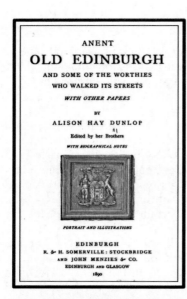

1. Title page of *Anent Old Edinburgh*, 1890
2. Letter from John Dunlop, published in The Scotsman, 1882
3. Memorial Gate to Alison Dunlop, Inverleith Park

STOCKBRIDGE AND THE REMOVING OF THE LANDMARKS

What has Stockbridge done? Of what crime or misdemeanour have its inhabitants been guilty that the scourge of civic change should fall so much more heavily on "our village" than on the rest of Edinburgh, and that twelve of our streets should have their well-worn names blotted from memory? We are a quiet people in Stockbridge, but we have an attachment to our native places and to our native streets? Concerning the largest alteration, which is to blot out six names, and substitute one new street - "Stockbridge Street". It is an act of supererogation to me to meddle with North West Circus Place at all.

Again, concerning our Brunswick Street, which is proposed to become an appendix of St Stephen Street , I only wish to remark that no one has known it more intimately that I have done for the last forty years, and during all that time I have never heard or known of any mistake occurring through its having a name-sister in town. Concerning Church Street, the intention to change its name into the degradation of India Lane is not easily understood, seeing there is a pair of Indias amongst our street nomenclature already. The contiguity of Stockbridge to India is not in any way remarkable and there is surely no startling resemblance among us to the dusky inhabitants of that very warm country to account for this inscrutable preference.

Church Street and Church Lane are the remains of old "Kirk gate" or kirk road from Granton and Stockbridge to the West Kirk when that church was the only place of worship in all its wide parish. Church Street retains traces of its name - Anglicised it is true - the more's the pity; but still intelligible enough to be a pleasant landmark to the archaeologist. In Church Street, too, David Roberts was born. Near his birthplace is that of Sir Henry Raeburn. If a new appellation was wanting could the street not have been named after either its gifted sons? Though had they been alive, both would have protested against such a change, albeit in their day, Church Lane was pleasantly famous for the smell of its sweet briar and wild roses on the June Sabbath days. So far I have been able to investigate Church Street is perhaps the oldest road in the suburbs of Edinburgh.

organising of international matches played there. In 1874 a major cricket match took place at the Grange ground when an all-England cricket team containing the top English players took on an Edinburgh team. Unusually, while the English team consisted of the usual eleven, the Edinburgh team had eighteen players! The match was played over two innings and the Edinburgh team lost by only 19 runs. The following year it was international rugby: 'The fifth international match according to the rugby rules, between teams representing England and Scotland, was played this afternoon at the Grange Cricket Club at Raeburn Place. The weather was fine and there was a large attendance of 6,000 spectators. After a stiff contest, the match ended in a draw.'

In 1878 John was elected as one of the three councillors to sit on the Town Council representing St Bernard's Ward and served on the council for many years. His passion for the area and things antiquarian led him to lead a revolt against proposed name changes to some of Stockbridge's streets in 1882. However, his protest was in vain and Brunswick Street was incorporated into St Stephen Street.

John and Alison moved to live at 32 Clarence Street in 1887 and Alison died there the year after. Her brothers edited a selection of her writings and had them published in 1889 as *Anent Old Edinburgh and some of the worthies who walked its streets.*' John never married and died in 1899.

The Scotsman reported on his funeral: 'The remains of the late Councillor J. C. Dunlop were yesterday interred in Warriston Cemetery amid numerous outward manifestations of sorrow and regret on the part of the citizens of Edinburgh; and more particularly on the part of the people of Stockbridge, in whose interests he laboured so untiringly and so successfully during many of the later years of his life. The Lord Provost, Magistrates, and Corporation attended the funeral in their public capacity, driving from the City Chambers in carriages to the house of the deceased, dressed in their robes of office, and attended by the mace and sword bearers and halberdiers. About fifty private carriages followed the funeral car drawn by two horses. As the procession to the cemetery moved slowly along, it was received with respectful silence by the large crowds that lined the streets. Shops on the route lowered their shutters, and the tramway traffic ceased till the carriages had passed.'

While there is no memorial to the Dunlops in St Stephen Street, they have two memorials in Inverleith Park. Alison's brothers paid for Inverleith Park's East Gate piers to be erected in her memory and further along in the park is a memorial drinking fountain set in a rough granite obelisk that the city erected in honour of John. The inscription on the base survives but not the water fountain.

AUSTRALIA'S CRACK SHOT

The Cairo Evening Mail has the following account of the wonderful work of an Australian marksman on the Gallipoli Peninsula, written by Private Frank Reed, another Australian Trooper.

W. E. Sing may be termed Australia's champion rifle shot, for during the time he was on Gallipoli he accounted for over 200 Turks. Of course, during enemy attacks he probably shot many more, but as a sniper he knows that over 200 fell owing to his excellent marksmanship. Sing's sniping methods were somewhat similar to those of the Turk; he played them at their own game, and beat then badly. His `posy' was so close to the Turkish trenches that their artillery rarely troubled him. He had three distinct targets that his mates, by tacit consent, left.to him. One was an enemy trench 360 yards away, another was a communication sap 600 yards off, the third was a track in a gully 1,000 yards distant. Comfortably ensconced in his nest Sing lay with a couple of telescopes focused on likely places. An officer lay near with another telescope. So afraid were the Turks of these unlucky spots that the patient sniper often lay a whole day without getting a glimpse the enemy. On other days the Turks (new troops probably) walked boldly into view and Sing toppled them over. He would exclaim: 'too easy to be called sport.' He never fired at a stretcher bearer or any the soldiers who were trying to rescue wounded Turks.

1. Newspaper report from The Globe, 17 January 1916
2. Elizabeth Stewart & Billy Sing, 1916
3. Certificate dated 26 November 1919 recording birth of Elizabeth's first child

Elizabeth Stewart & Billy Sing

George and Clementina Stewart moved into the house that was now renamed and renumbered 45 St Stephen Street around 1917 with their children. George was working as a merchant seaman. Their eldest daughter, Elizabeth, then 20, was working as a waitress in a Leith restaurant, where she met a thirty-year-old soldier, Billy Sing. He was Australian, the son of a Chinese father and an English mother. Billy was on leave before being posted back to France, having just left hospital after being wounded in action on the Somme.

Before the war Sing had proven a highly skilled rifle marksman and at Gallipoli in 1915 served as a sniper. Such was his proficiency that he is estimated to have killed over 200 German soldiers and he became dubbed 'The Assassin' by his fellow soldiers. He then served in France and in 1916 was awarded the Distinguished Conduct Medal. His achievement was lauded in the British press but it is quite likely that Elizabeth knew nothing of his sharp-shooting fame when they met.

Why he was in Leith on his leave remains a mystery, but what is certain is that he fell head over heels in love with Elizabeth. Just five or six weeks later, having had his leave extended, he married her at 68 Pilrig Street, the home of the Reverend James Rouse, a United Free Church minister. Days later Billy was back fighting in France. In early 1918 he was wounded in action again and after recovering was given leave to see Elizabeth. He travelled to Edinburgh in July and spent a short time with his young wife.

A few weeks later he sailed for Australia, having promised Elizabeth he would obtain permission for her to join him there. This he gained and although he wrote to her with the arrangements for her travel he received no reply. Nor was there any answer from Elizabeth to any of his numerous subsequent letters.

In 1919 Elizabeth became pregnant and moved back to live with her family in St Stephen Street. In September she gave birth to a daughter, Mary Millar Stewart. Although the birth certificate names William Sing as the father, he evidently could not have been, but who the father was is not known. In 1922 Elizabeth met an Australian merchant seaman, (Theodore) Mark Malmborg and their son was born in May 1923 and also named Theodore. In 1925 Mark arranged for Elizabeth and the two children to travel to Australia and Elizabeth Stewart/Sing arrived in Sydney under a new name: Mrs Gladys Malmborg. Mark died in 1971 and Elizabeth/Gladys in 1977. Billy Sing died in relative poverty and obscurity in Brisbane in 1943, never knowing that his wife had been living in Australia since 1923 under an assumed name.

1. Advert for sale of the tenement on corner with Clarence Street, 1850
2. Douglas Haig, c.1870
3. Advert, 1842
4. Advert 1846

Residents of 1 / 97 St Stephen Street

When built, the ground floor of the tenement on the south east corner of St Stephen Street and Clarence Street was the only house in St Stephen Street, thus number 1, but was renumbered 97 when Brunswick Street was incorporated into St Stephen Street.

Although the ground floor flat was part of the corner tenement in Clarence Street, as it was entered from St Stephen Street that was, in all but name at the time, an extension to the overcrowded and unfashionable Brunswick Street. Also between the tenement and St Stephen's Church were nothing but timber yards and other workplaces. This may have been why few residents stayed more than a few years.

The first occupant from 1840 was Mary Veitch, the young widow of Hugh Forester Veitch of Stewartfield House, Newhaven Road and her son, James, who advertised from the house as an insurance agent. Hugh had been the Town Clerk of Leith before his death in 1837. Although Mary inherited Stewartfield House, she had been left in 'straitened circumstances' and leased the large house and moved to the Stockbridge flat. The family's reduced financial circumstance may have been the reason for Mary's nineteen-year-old daughter, Rachel - reputed to be 'the most beautiful woman in Scotland' - marrying the 37-year-old John Haig. He was extremely wealthy, being the head of the family owning the successful Haig & Haig whisky distillery. Over the following twenty years Rachel bore many children to her alcoholic husband, of which eleven survived into adulthood. Her last child, Douglas, was just eighteen and at university when both his parents died within a year of each other. Although none of his relations had been in the army, Douglas chose that career and achieved outstanding success. When Field Marshall Douglas Haig died in 1928 his funeral was a day of national mourning in recognition of his role as commander of the British Forces in the First World War. After three years Mary and her family moved to the more stylish York Place.

Mrs Dickson taught foreign languages from the house for a few years. and then, in 1856 Lieutenant John O'Neill moved in with his family. He was the Staff Adjutant for North Britain and thus the principal administrative staff officer for the forces in Edinburgh. This was a difficult time for him, as one of his duties was overseeing the regulations regarding the billeting of soldiers and this was causing disquiet in the city. For many years there had been unrest at the practice of billeting soldiers upon private families and in 1857 the law was changed. Now the obligation for billeting was transferred to hotel-keepers and publicans in the city. Understandably, this did not go down well with Edinburgh's hospitality businesses. 'One hotel-keeper, very far from being the largest in the city,

1. Advert, 1846
2. Advert, 1900
3. Advert, 1901
4. Ken Stott as Inspector Rebus on India Street steps. 1990s

51

has been enjoined to provide no less a number than 478 billets in the last six months.' Many refused and O'Neill was kept busy taking them to court. Perhaps all this worry took its toll, for he died in the house in 1859.

The next residents were Lewis and Amelia Mitchell, and their three unmarried daughters in their late twenties and their son, a divinity student. Lewis was a retired Royal Navy Commander in his early sixties. When young, his ship took part in the Battle of Algiers in 1816 that was fought to release Christians enslaved there and Lewis received eight wounds in the battle.

The Mitchells moved to Raeburn Place and the house was taken by a young widow, Gertrude Campbell. She had been living in Stornoway with her husband Patrick Campbell, the Inspecting Commander of the Coast Guard, until his early death. She had three children under ten. She was the daughter of Captain Joseph Barnes of the Royal Artillery and his widow came to live with Gertrude to help look after the children. Two of the children died in India. John, had joined the army and was just 22 when, serving in India, he died of cholera. More happily, the eldest daughter, Olivia, married Campbell Primrose, an officer serving in Madras, at Mangalore, India. She had eight children and lived in India until her death in 1921.

Adam Pearson purchased the house and let it as he lived in Blackford Road. He was a retired leather merchant and around 1860 had been a member of the City Council. In 1880 he was declared bankrupt and although sixty-nine-years old absconded to America and a warrant for his arrest was issued. Whether he was ever traced is not known. By then the house had been sold to Elizabeth Moffat.

Henry and Christina Brown and their three sons and three daughters moved here from 77 St Stephen Place. He was a cabinetmaker, while Christina worked as a dressmaker, and they took in boarders – 'comfortable sitting room and bedroom, piano and bath, to let'. Their eldest son, Henry, who was married and working as a tailor, was killed in the war in 1917 while fighting with the Scottish Rifles, and the husband of the Browns' daughter Minnie, also died in the last week of the war.

In 1931 the flat was advertised for £600 and bought by Mrs Christian Murray. Since 1900 the house had suffered from structural problems and by 1970 these were so serious that a large vertical crack ran through the tenement's front wall. Fortunately, thanks to restoration work by Robert Hurd & Partners, it was saved from demolition.

In the late 1990s the house had a starring role in the television adaptation of Ian Rankin's *Rebus* novels starring Ken Stott, its interior representing Rebus's fictional flat in Arden Street, Marchmont. In 2021 the flat sold for over £770,000.

1. George Adamson
2. Thomas Adamson
3. Royal Scots resting at Leith after mobilisation, August 1914

First World War

Within days of Britain declaring war on Germany on 4 August 1914 thousands joined the armed forces, including many husbands and sons from St Stephen Street. As well as posters calling for men to join up to fight, adverts appeared seeking skilled workers: 'Tradesmen required for the army.' Among the trades listed were copper-smiths, electricians, blacksmiths and farriers. The pay was good and a bounty of £5 was offered to those joining up, so within weeks of the war's start, the street's businesses were depleted of experienced male employees. And a great many never returned.

Among the first to volunteer was 25-year-old George Adamson, who was working as a tailor. His parents, John and Maggie Adamson, had recently moved to Edinburgh from Galashiels and rented a flat at number 47. George joined a new battalion of the Royal Scots that was being raised in Edinburgh and in May 1915 the battalion arrived in France. In that same month, George's younger brother Thomas enlisted in the Cameron Highlanders. On 14 July 1916 Thomas took part in the Battle of Bazentin Ridge, part of the Battle of the Somme, and on the third day of chaotic bloody fighting was reported missing in action. George survived many horrific battles but in July 1917 at The Third Battle of Ypres, also known as the Battle of Passchendaele, he too was reported missing. Neither brother's body was ever found.

The Lockies at number 136 also lost two sons. When the war began, George was 20 and working as a telegraph messenger, while his brother, Thomas (15) was still at school. George joined the Royal Scots and died in the fighting at Gallipoli in Turkey in June 1915. Thomas was conscripted into the Royal Scots as soon as he had passed his 18th birthday and was killed in the Battle of Amiens in August 1915.

Men who had worked in the street also died. By an ill-fated coincidence John O'Brien who had been employed at the pawnbroker's shop at number 10 was killed in Gallipoli in the same attack and on the same day as George Lockie.

When the war began Italy was a partner in the Triple Alliance with Germany and Austria-Hungary, but decided to remain neutral. However, for Italians living in Britain, neutrality was not an option and Joseph, the son of Angelo and Enrichetta Vaghi, who had come from Italy around 1910 and lived at number 112, joined the Scottish Horse Mounted Brigade. Like many he lied about his age – being a year younger than the eighteen-year-old limit – and the army colluded in the pretence. In the early part of the war Joseph took part in coastal defence in Northumbria and from there sent a postcard home: 'Dear Mother, I am sorry for not writing before but I could not as I have been living in trenches for the past

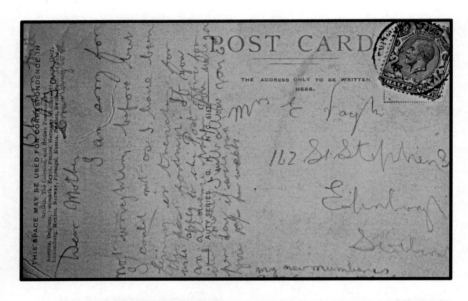

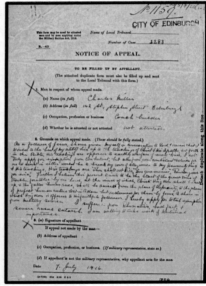

1. Postcard sent by Joseph Vaghi to his mother, 1914 (First World War
Poetry Digital Archive)
2. Joseph Vaghi
3. Appeal Form by Charlie Miller, 1916

fortnight. If you will apply to the Post Office for an allowance paper you will get my money. I will allow you (6d?) per day - it will run you 10/- (ten shillings) per week.' In August 1915 his brigade sailed for Gallipoli in Turkey and on 2 September took part in dismounted landings at Suvla Bay. Joseph died on the fifth day of the battle, barely eighteen.

The following month another resident in the tenement, Alexander Caw (23), a sergeant with the King's Own Scottish Borderers, was killed in France leaving his young wife a widow. These two deaths must have caused concern among younger male residents of number 142 that they might be called up as it was clear the army was going to need more men. So it proved for the following January the Military Service Act was passed, imposing conscription on all single men aged between 18 and 41, but exempting the medically unfit, clergymen, teachers and certain classes of industrial worker.

Three brothers, James, William and Donald McDonald, who lived in the house tried to evade conscription and were arrested. They were each fined £2 and handed over to the military. Their fates are unknown. Charlie Miller who lived in the tenement received his call up papers in June 1916. He was thirty-years-old, married with two children and worked at Croall Coachworks. There were many firms that sought exemption for men they claimed to be essential to their operation, although such appeals seldom were successful. As Charlie was employed repairing and building motor vehicles the firm would have known they would not win an appeal for his exemption as his skills were very much in demand by the army.

However, the Military Service Act gave legal recognition to individual conscience - Britain being the first country to do so - and Charlie applied for an exemption as a conscientious objector. He was a recent convert to the International Bible Students Association (later renamed the Jehovah Witnesses) and the group forbade members to fight in wars. In his application to the Military Tribunal Charlie wrote: 'I not only apply for exemption from combatant, but also from non-combatant service for me to assist in either would be to break my vows of allegiance to my Heavenly King.' He added that he suffered from rheumatism. Just a few months earlier the International Bible Students Association had written to the Government seeking exemption from active service for all its members as had been agreed for other religious groups, such as the Quakers but were unsuccessful. Charlie's application carried various letters of support. One from William Quarrier who founded the Orphan Homes of Scotland stated: 'Charlie Miller has always borne a Christian character. He worked in connection with our City Home Mission for eight years.'

The Tribunal ruled that Charlie was exempted from combatant service only. So, Charlie appealed, this time on the basis of his rheumatism,

OBSERVATIONS OF MILITARY REPRESENTATIVE.

[NOTE—In cases to which Military Representative assents, he should write "I assent to the application." Where he objects to the application he should state briefly the reasons for his objection. If an absolute Certificate is applied for and the Military Representative considers that only a conditional or temporary Certificate should be granted he should state his reasons.]

9. Decision of the Tribunal. *To be signed and dated. If exemption is granted it should be stated whether it is to be absolute, conditional (in which case the conditions to be entered on the certificate should be stated) or temporary (in which case the time for which the exemption is granted should be stated).*

Grant exemption from combatant service only on the ground

That he has a conscientious objection to the undertaking of combatant service.

4/7/16.   Thomas Hunter
                                   Clerk

EXOTIC SPECIES AND RACES OF VARIOUS SPECIES.

Considerable numbers of tree seeds of various species, mainly from Japan and N.America were sown in Inverleith nursery during the year with satisfactory results except that one lot of Pinus ponderosa which took a long time to germinate, was eaten by birds and mice.

Seed of various races of Pinus sylvestris and of P. contorta were sown.

1. Decision of appeal by Charlie Miller, July 1916
2. Scottish Horse regiment
3. Forestry Commission Research Project at Inverleith Nursery where Charles Duncan worked, 1923

enclosing a letter from Dr Robert Mowat stating that he had treated Charlie for the complaint for the last eighteen months. Yet again, the appeal was rejected. What then happened to Charlie is not known. It is likely that like other conscientious objectors he would have been ordered to join the Non-Combatant Corps (NCC). This was a military unit in which men worked in support roles that did not involve fighting or the use of arms. However, if , like others, Charlie had remained true to his stand that he could not support the war effort in any way then he would have been severely treated. Such men were imprisoned, some threatened with court martial and execution, while a few were taken to France and simply disappeared.

Of course many of those who fought in the war survived, although a number suffered afterwards from physical and/or mental disabilities. When war was declared Charles Duncan was 21. He lived with his family at number 116 and worked as a gardener for his father, who managed a nursery in Inverleith Row. He had been dating Mary Conkey, a 26-year-old baker's assistant whose father worked as a cable car conductor, and, like many young couples when war was declared, they decided to wed. On 24 September 1914 they were married by the minister of Dean Church and Mary moved in with the Duncan family for the duration of the war. Charles served with the Royal Field Artillery as a gunner, fighting in France for three years. Charles was wounded in July 1918 and recovered in the Scottish General Hospital in Aberdeen. On his discharge he returned to live in St Stephen Street with his wife and family, and continued to work at Inverleith Nursery as a gardener.

In early 1915 Rev. Lauchlan Watt, the minister of St Stephen's Church since 1911, went to France as a chaplain with the Gordon Highlanders in the 7th Division. He was a skilled bagpipe player and would keep up men's morale by playing familiar Scottish tunes, earning himself the nickname of 'the Piping Padre'. Alongside his musical and spiritual care for the soldiers, he wrote articles and published poems about the war. In spite of the horrors he must have witnessed, his view of the conflict echoed the patriotic fervour of the time. In one article for The Scotsman he wrote: 'There never was so great an opportunity for a spiritual uprising as that which is offered by this war. The men are pressed on either side with the vast issues of life and death and eternal things. They are hungry for the bread of life. No matter what the cynic may say, they have passed through a really great awakening.' Watt had further spells in France, acting as an army chaplain and writing about the soldiers' experiences.

Two women from St Stephen's Church also went to France in 1915. Miss Guy and Miss Stewart volunteered to join the work being carried out by the Young Men's Christian Association (YMCA) aiding soldiers at the front. The two women spent six months close to the front line providing

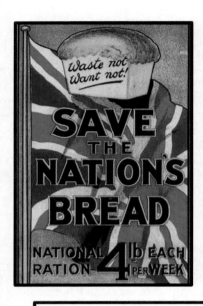

Waste not
Want not!

SAVE
THE
NATION'S
BREAD

NATIONAL RATION 4 lb EACH PER WEEK

MS.1988-15/2.a

S.E. 30
RETAILER'S   SUGAR TICKET.

This Ticket is issued under the authority of the Food
Controller by:—
ST. CUTH. COOP
(Retailer's Name and Address, written or rubber-stamped.)
ASSOC. LTD
62 HAMILTON PL.

in respect of the person named in Part A on the back,
being a member of the household of:—
(Householder's Name) Wm M. Murray
and must be produced to the Retailer upon every purchase
of sugar in respect of that person.
NOTE.—The space above for the householder's name and Part A
on the back must be filled up immediately upon the issue of this
Ticket, and in any case before it is produced to the Retailer.

TRANSFER, ON REMOVAL, Etc.
If the person named on the back removes altogether or
ceases to be a member of the above-mentioned household,
Part B on the back should be filled up and the Ticket
should then be taken to a Post Office.
59752) Wt. 4615. 10/17. John Corah & Son. (E2033.)   F.22.

SHOPS, BUSINESS PREMISES, &c.
FREDERICK STREET, 39.—Basement shop, ad-
joining George Street, 3 apartments .... ..:.... 17 0
PITT STREET, 10A.—Front shop and back room.. 17 0
ST STEPHEN STREET.—Several good shops at
moderate rents.

1. Poster, 1914
2. Sugar ration ticket, 1918
3. Advert for empty shops that
appeared repeatedly in 1916 and
1917
4. Women in factory, c.1917.

recreational support for soldiers that were convalescing. 'Miss Guy has written to say that a splendid gift is material for reading. Any stories or illustrated magazines will be most gratefully received.'

While the recurring loss of relations and neighbours must have negatively affected those who lived in St Stephen Street, in the early days the main concern for most was a sudden shortage of supplies as panic buying ensued: 'Excessive purchases are being made by needlessly alarmed customers whose unreasonable conduct cannot be too strongly deprecated.' One unexpected immediate scarcity was coins. 'Reluctance on the part of traders to give change for paper money is being experienced in Edinburgh. This shortage of small change is the result of the closing of banks making it impossible for shops to secure silver and copper coins.' Later, there were shortages of certain foods and by late 1917 official food rationing was phased in. In February 1918 Edinburgh distributed meat ration cards that restricted individuals to purchasing meat each week to the value of 1s6d.

From 1915 until well after the war's end, the street suffered a severe decline in trade. Newspapers regularly advertised empty shops in the street to let; some had closed because the men who worked in them - shoemakers, watchmakers, etc .- were called up, while others found it hard to survive due to a decline in trade as families lost their main breadwinner. The largest business in the street, the printing firm, Waddie and Company, suffered from a shortage of skilled labour and regularly advertised for employees. One positive consequence was that jobs that hitherto had been a male preserve opened up to women and Waddie advertised: 'Girls wanted for ruling and printing department.'

It is not known how many men from St Stephen Street fought, but at least thirty men who had parents or wives living in the street were killed. Almost 790 male members of the congregation of St Stephen's Church fought in the war and of those, 152 died.

Extract from *The Reapers* by Rev. Lauchlan Watt
Written on 2 July 1916, after the first day of the Battle of the Somme.

Tired, so many, with reaping,
Tired with treading the grain,
Still they lie, in their sleeping,
Low in the Valley of Pain.
Never again to be quaffing
The joy of life, like wine;
Never again to be laughing
In youth's glad hour divine.

Birds shall sing in the branches,
Children dance by the shore;
But they who shared the red reaping
Shall come back nevermore.
Let whoso can forget them,
Walking life's noisy ways;
We who have looked on the Reapers
Go quietly, all our days.

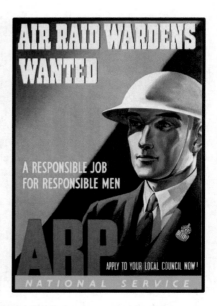

LOOK OUT IN THE BLACK-OUT

- Before you leave your house, railway station or office, let your eyes get used to the dark
- Before you cross a road, look both ways
- To stop a bus, hold up something white. Do not flash a torch
- Before you get off a bus, tram or train, wait until it has stopped and step carefully

AIR RAID WARDENS WANTED

A RESPONSIBLE JOB FOR RESPONSIBLE MEN

ARP

APPLY TO YOUR LOCAL COUNCIL NOW!

NATIONAL SERVICE

1. Poster, 1939
2. Poster, 1939
3. Children being evacuated, 1939

Second World War

Almost a year before the Second World War began, preparations were being made for the feared impact of bombing and gas attacks on the city. The Chief Air Raid Warden for Edinburgh called for volunteers at a meeting of ratepayers of St Stephen's Ward: 'It must not be supposed that an air raid warden is a highly expert person. What we need are willing citizens who know their neighbourhood, and can satisfy themselves that by the end of the week local people will have their proper gas respirator, and know the way to the nearest shelter. They need to be cool, calm, collected persons, who know what to do and where to go. Under the headings of wardens, first aid workers, auxiliary firemen, and drivers, we need 270 men, of whom we already have 180. Tomorrow 300 men are beginning in the public parks to make trenches for that percentage of the population who might not be able to find accommodation near their own homes.' A local fire warden's post was opened at number 134 and the fire wardens were issued with special helmets and stirrup pumps, and an air-raid shelter was established in the basement of St Stephen's Church to accommodate 200 people.

By the summer of 1939 with war almost certain, the government issued a pamphlet, *Advice to Animal Owners*: 'If at all possible, send or take your household animals into the country in advance of an emergency....If you cannot place them in the care of neighbours, it really is kindest to have them destroyed.' Although vets and animal protection organisations were incensed and made appeals to owners not to put down their pets, in one day in early September Broughton Dog and Cat Home put down 200 dogs and cats. Also the evacuation of children began and Elspeth Wallace who lived at number 126 was sent to Inverness. As well as children and pets disappearing from the street, so were the many men and women who joined the armed forces, again leading to worker shortages for many local businesses.

One newspaper wrote: 'Darkened streets, citizens carrying gas masks to their daily tasks, broadcast announcements of war news, hoardings displaying proclamations - all these ought to impress every single person that the nation is at war and that every household has its own part to play.' The blackout caused many accidents. While it was usually traffic collisions, in November 1939 one man died when in the pitch black he fell into the sunk basement area of number 19.

While Scottish Italians had fought for Britain in the First World War, this was forgotten when Italy joined Germany against the Allied Forces. Italians were interned and their shops in the city attacked and looted. In June 1940 James Rooney, a rubber worker, who lived at number 32 appeared in court with two others charged with having broken into a shop

1. Rationing, 1943
2. 'We have no bananas' sign, c.1942
3. V.E. day in Princes Street Gardens, May 1945
4. Thomas Peck Hunter
5. Children rush to the sweet shops, 5 February 1953

run by an Italian family and stolen goods and cash. 'Rooney's father said he realised the crime was a serious one, but he thought it was a case of misplaced patriotism. At the present time everyone was in a high state of nerves and it did not take much to upset people, especially after Italy entered the war (loud applause from the public gallery). Sheriff Jameson said he could not agree that breaking into a shop and stealing goods was patriotism. The cowardly sacking of Italian shops was just plain theft. It was a very un-British thing to do. He fined Rooney £2.'

As the war dragged on the main concern for most living in the street was a shortage of food, and rationing was introduced. As shortages increased, long queues became commonplace and the rationing of petrol led to the reappearance of horse-drawn vehicles. It was not until the early 1950s that rationing came to an end. Fortunately, the feared gas attacks never materialised and the street was unaffected by the limited bombing, although five years after the war ended four local boys found a live shell and began throwing it to each other in the stair of 24 Clarence Street. It exploded, injuring all four, one seriously.

Of course again many local families lost loved ones. Two sons of Mr and Mrs Mason who lived at 9 St Stephen Place died. John Mason (29) was serving in the Royal Naval Patrol Service on board HMS Ebor Wyke when it was sunk by a German submarine in May 1945, and Andrew (19) died from wounds received in the fighting at Arnhem in May 1944 while serving with the Airborne Division of the Kings Own Scottish Borderers. Mary Hardie at number 65 was left a young widow when her husband, Charles, died in 1942 while serving in the R.A.F.

Thomas Peck Hunter was 16 and working as an apprentice stationer at Waddie & Co when war was declared. Being too young to join the army, he volunteered in the Home Guard. In May 1942 he was conscripted and enlisted as a Royal Commando Marine. On 2 April 1945 he was fighting in Italy: 'Corporal Hunter, who was in charge of a Bren gun section, offered himself as a target to save his troop. Seizing the Bren gun, he charged alone across 200 yards of open ground under most intense fire towards a group of houses where three MG 42 machine-guns were lodged. So determined was his charge that the enemy soldiers were demoralised and six gunners surrendered. The remainder fled. Hunter cleared the house, changing magazines as he ran and continued to draw enemy fire until most of the troop had reached cover. Hunter then was killed.' He was posthumously decorated with the Victoria Cross and in 2002 a memorial in his honour was erected outside Edinburgh's Ocean Terminal.

Although the war ended in May 1945 it was not until 5 February 1953 that all could celebrate for on that day sweetie rationing ended. The BBC reported: "Children all over Britain have been emptying out their piggy banks and heading straight for the nearest sweet shop.

Collected by Agnes Ord, St Stephen's School,
Edinburgh, for orphans at Calcutta   .   L.0   0   9
Mr Tawse's class, St Stephen's Sabbath
School, for the Jews   .   .   .   0   1   6
Collected at a missionary meeting of the chil-
dren attending St Stephen's School, Edin-
burgh   0   8   3½
Contribution for St Stephen's mission at
Gaspara (!) by the class taught by Mr Gourlie
in St Stephen's Sabbath School   .   .   0   9   0½"

1. Open bible sculpture on the top of St Stephen's School
2. Newspaper report of monies raised from pupils for good causes, 1846
3. Window above school's door

St Stephen's School

Until the Education (Scotland) Act 1872 introduced universal education for all children aged from five to 13, many children from poor families – especially girls – had little, if any, schooling. Although a boys' school, Edinburgh Academy, opened in 1824 in Henderson Row, it was too expensive for parents in Brunswick Street. While it is likely that a few children attended one of the private schools dotted around the area and others received limited schooling at the St Stephen's Church Sabbath School, it was not until the opening of St Stephen's School in 1836 that most local working class children could obtain an education.

The school was built by St Stephen's Church, with the congregation contributing £800 and the balance of funds to buy the land and erect the building coming from a government grant. The school was designed by George Smith and when opened consisted of: 'three floors, each forming a spacious room for the accommodation of a separate class; the classes forming a boys' school, a girls' school, and an infant school, comprising about 400 children, belonging to the poorer classes of the parish.' Although the building has a sculpture of an open bible on its facade stating, 'Those that seek me early shall find me', and was partly funded by St Stephen's Church, it was not a formal church school, and was open to children of all religious denominations.

Evening classes also were held in the school for young men; the subjects taught were English Grammar, Religious and General Knowledge, English Composition, Writing, Arithmetic, Geography, Book-keeping, and the Elements of Algebra.

Around 1839 William Lambie Nelson was appointed headmaster, and he and his family lived at number 50. At the time William was a divinity student at Edinburgh University. In 1853, having been ordained, he left to become a minister in Musselburgh and later moved to Australia at the invitation of the Sydney Presbytery. In 1860 he was elected to the Queensland Legislative Assembly but disqualified due to his being a religious minister. However, his son, Hugh Nelson, who had been a pupil at St Stephen's School, was elected to the Queensland Legislative Assembly twenty years later and became Queensland's premier in 1893.

Alexander Smith served as Head Teacher from 1853 until the school's closure in 1890, and Marion Miellan was mistress of the girls' school from 1855 till her death in 1881. In 1843 there was a major schism in the Church of Scotland and many churches broke away to become the Free Protesting Church of Scotland. Two of the school's teachers, Jane Hunter and Fanny Crone, joined the Free Church but as St Stephen's Church remained in the established church, both women were dismissed. There was an outcry but the school refused to reinstate them. Fortunately, the

1. William Lambie Nelson
2. Hugh Nelson
3. Edinburgh school pupils, 1890s (thanks to Kathleen Hamilton)

sacked teachers were employed at a new Free Church School in the Assembly Hall, Canonmills.

In 1897 Hugh Nelson visited Britain and was a guest at a reception in the City Chambers along with a number of former pupils of St Stephen's School. One was the Edinburgh Councillor, William Slater Brown who recounted his early days: 'My father worked as a tailor for a small business in Stockbridge. I was the second of a family of six, and at an early age had to face myself for the battle of life. My little schooling was obtained at St Stephen's School before I left as I had to begin work at an early age.' Brown was apprenticed as a cabinetmaker and by the 1890s his firm, W S Brown & Sons had a sawmill and timber-yard in St Stephen Street and an 'artistic furnishing warehouse' at 65 George Street. In 1909 he was elected Lord Provost of Edinburgh and knighted in 1910.

Whether Clement Gunn - another former pupil - attended the reception is not known. He was a sickly baby when his father died in 1861, aged only 36, leaving his widow with six children. 'Three things pulled me through: the grace of God, a mother's love and sack whey (sherry with weak milk and sugar)'. He was dux of St Stephen's School and went on to train as a doctor at Edinburgh University, studying alongside Arthur Conan Doyle. Gunn set up as a general practitioner in Peebles, and wrote many books on the Burgh and District, including *Leaves from the Life of a Country Doctor*.

The school year ended with examinations. In 1861: 'These were made on three several days in the presence of the kirk-session, of members of the church, and of many of the parents of the children. The result was admirably illustrative of the talent, skill, and success of Mr Smith, Miss McLellan and Miss Leslie, the teachers, whose diligence and faithfulness merit the highest praise. The boys and girls were, on the evening of the last day of examination, gathered together to their annual soiree, when they spent a very pleasant evening. The schools are supported partly by very moderate school fees, and partly by the continued liberality of St Stephen's congregation.' Given that it was recorded that around 500 children attended the school at this time, the fact that only three teachers were employed is astonishing.

As well as introducing universal education for children aged from 5 to 13 years, the Education (Scotland) Act 1872 created local School Boards throughout the country. These took over most church schools and oversaw the building of many grand, purpose-built schools. St Stephen's School continued to function independently until 1890, at which point the Edinburgh School Board decided that there was no need for the school as sufficient accommodation existed elsewhere for all the pupils in the district. The building then became residential.

1. William Forbes Skene by Sir George Reid, c.1888
2. St Vincent's Hall. originally built as the Stockbridge Working Men's Club
3. Advert, 1933
4. Poster for Dance For All

Stockbridge Working Men's Club / St Vincent's Hall

This building was not built by St Vincent's Chapel as its hall as is commonly thought, but rather was erected for the Stockbridge Working Men's Club. In 1866 a number of St Stephen's Ward councillors and others raised the idea of establishing a Working Men's Institute in the area, similar to those that existed in other districts of the city, and erected the hall. A newspaper report of its opening in March 1867 described it: 'The building, which is entered by a few steps from Brunswick Street, contains on the main floor two large rooms to be used as a reading-room and a room for draught-playing and other amusements; these rooms are divided by a partition, the removal of which furnishes a commodious lecture-hall with a gallery at the further end. On the ground floor are the bagatelle-room and the usual conveniences. The whole building is comfortable, well-lighted, and admirably fitted for the purpose.'

A programme of well-attended lectures were delivered in the hall in its first year and included *Rambles in Russia* 'illustrated by photographs of buildings in St Petersburg and Moscow, exhibited by the oxy-hydrogen light.' There also was a series of concerts: 'The programme was interesting and varied, consisting chiefly of Scotch songs, duets, glees, and quartets. The pieces were all skilfully rendered, and elicited the hearty applause of the audience.'

However, the Working Men's Club had a short life and around 1870 the building was purchased by Dr William Skene, who also purchased St Vincent's Chapel and gifted both buildings to the congregation. Although used by the Chapel, up to 1905 it also was let to a congregation of Wesleyan Methodists and, later, Baptists for their services. The hall also was hired out for a range of events, from political meetings to social events. In May 1879 the Stockbridge Conservative Association held its inaugural meeting in the hall, while in 1948 the hall was the venue for a meeting of the relatively young Scottish National Party. Social events included 'a pleasant evening for Grocers' Assistants - all shop assistants and lady friends cordially invited.'

The hall was bought by William Mowat Thomson in 1976. Although Thomson trained as a dancer he decided to employ his skills in encouraging others to dance and opened The Theatre School of Dance and Drama – today Dance for All. Thomson was well-connected in the dance and theatre worlds, and performers such as David Bowie and Lindsay Kemp gave classes at number 106. However, there were earlier links with dance. In the early 1900s Mr Maxwell advertised Juvenile Dance Classes and Mr Clark promoted Saturday evening dances in the hall.

1. St Stephen's Church Mission Hall
2. Review of a concert, 1940
3. A member of the Boy Reserves, 1917

St Stephen's Church Mission Hall

This building was designed by Sydney Mitchell in early Gothic style for St Stephen's Church as their Mission Hall and opened in 1883. It contained several rooms, including a library and a large classroom on the ground floor and a hall seating 600 on the second. In 1907 a Men's and Lad's Social Club was established in the hall. 'In declaring the club open Dr Grant spoke of the need of the Church taking an interest in the amusements of the people. The premises consist of three large rooms on the ground flat, one of which is to be used as a billiard and smoking room, whilst the other two are reserved for games and reading. A plentiful supply of papers, and magazines were displayed upon the tables and these, coupled with the bright fires, formed a most attractive picture. In the large hall upstairs on Monday and Thursday evenings gymnastic classes will be held. Equipment has been purchased and a trained instructor engaged, together providing the most up to-date gymnasium in Stockbridge. The club meets' every night from 7.30 to 10.30, and on Sunday evenings a special men's service is to be held, which will he addressed by some of the most prominent Edinburgh laymen.'

From the early 1900s the church ran a Young Men's Guild. In 1924 Captain Campbell, author of *Private Spud Tamson* delivered a lecture to the Guild members promoting the Empire. 'We must rouse the wanderlust - the love of the open road.' He promoted a new scheme established by the British and Canadian Governments that sought to entice 3,000 families to 'pioneer in the fair Dominion'. The scheme offered assisted passages and guaranteed that land, including livestock and equipment, would be sold to the settlers at reasonable cost. Campbell estimated that the average cost of a farm and its live stock would be about £800 to £1,300, and said that any families selected that were unable to find this sum in cash would be eligible for a loan. Whether any of the young men rushed home and convinced their family to head for the wide open spaces of Canada is not known.

The church also had companies of Boys Brigade and Boy Reserves (for juniors and later renamed the Life Boys). The Boys Brigade was created by Sir William Alexander Smith in Glasgow in 1883 with the aim: "The advancement of Christ's kingdom among Boys and the promotion of habits of Obedience, Reverence, Discipline, Self-respect and all that tends towards a true Christian manliness." The movement quickly spread and by the early 1890s was international. 'An interesting display, comprising saluting the flag, physical training, games, and signalling, was given in St Stephen's Mission Hall last night by the Boy Reserves.'

The hall continued to be used for church meetings and other parochial business until being sold around 2000 and converted into flats.

1. Horse-cart, c.1900
2. A meeting of cabmen, c.1880s

Transport

In the 19th century the sight, sound and smell of horses would have been an integral part of life in the street. Horse drawn vehicles would have rattled in and out, delivering beer, coal and other goods, and the occasional fire would have brought the horse-drawn fire engine clattering to the blaze.

While the majority of drivers treated their animals well, there were instances of horses being maltreated, especially through being forced to pull overloaded carts. In 1879 Alexander Calder, a dairyman living in St Stephen Street was fined 25s for 'working a horse which was lame from ringbone.' Dangerous and drunken driving were just as common in the days of horse-drawn vehicles. In 1858: 'Robert Wilson was charged with driving three horses attached to an omnibus in a furious and reckless manner down North West Circus Place to Stockbridge. A girl who was standing with a number of other children was knocked down and only escaped death by a kind of miracle.' David Spowart from number 19 pleaded guilty in 1887 to have been 'the worse of liquor' when he drove his horse and van recklessly. When drunk driving led to an accident it was usually the horses that came off worse.

A number of cabmen lived in the street over the years and in 1874: 'A meeting of about 200 cabmen was held near St Stephen's Church on Saturday night at eleven o'clock to consider what action they would take in consequence of the proprietors not having complied with their demand for a minimum weekly wage and one Sunday in two off.' Twenty years earlier the Church of Scotland had called for cabmen to be banned from working any Sunday: 'The cabmen state that their average time on watch and work, from Monday morning to Saturday night, is seventeen hours a-day, and on Sabbath are on the stand from nine in the morning till nine at night. Their toil has nothing intellectual about it, nothing to excite their faculties; but very much to weary, to deaden, to degrade, and to drive to unlawful stimulants. They are chained to their stand in the summer's heat and the winter's cold. They are banished from their own homes - from their wives and families - banished from the usual opportunities of intellectual and spiritual improvement. They hear the Sabbath-bell; but they cannot join in the Sabbath song.' There were others who argued that the horses also deserved one day's rest.

One St Stephen Street cabbie, John Gibson, drove a gentleman from the Caledonian Station to lodgings and as the man had no change, went upstairs with him so he could get change to pay the fare. Five minutes later, he came down to discover his hansom cab was gone. A woman informed him that two policemen had driven off with it to Leith. He rushed to the police station to reclaim his cab, only to be charged with

1. Horse-drawn omnibus, c.1900
2. Cable tram in Kerr Street (tenements on the left were demolished in 1960s), c.1910.

having left an unattended vehicle. Leaving unattended horses could be dangerous: in 1903, John Murray , a carter, was given a cash award for managing to stop a runaway horse in St Stephen Street 'at very great risk, the horse being at full gallop, and the difficulty and danger of bringing it to a stop very great.'

The first horse-drawn omnibus between Stockbridge and Newington, directly crossing through the city, was introduced around 1839 by Thomas Thorburn, who owned a draper's shop in North West Circus Place. The coach started from each end every half hour, the fare being 3d. In the 1870s horse drawn trams were introduced. These were pulled by two horses, although on the hill up from Stockbridge four or five horses were needed to pull the heavy trams. 'Trace boys' were employed to assist by leading, and pulling, the struggling horses and having helped get the tram to the top of the hill, ran back down to wait for the next one. In 1898 Frank Lewis, aged 18, who lived at number 10 above the pawnshop, was employed in this way. He and two others had taken tram horses off for a ride and ended up in court charged with 'recklessly and furiously riding tram horses in Lothian Road'. The boys were jailed for two days.

In 1890 a cable tram service was introduced between Comely Bank and Princes Street. Its route crossed the bridge and then continued up Circus Place and Howe Street. This was a tricky route to cable as it traversed 28 curves over its 2.5 miles, and ascended 173 feet. The cables ran from the powerhouse in Henderson Row, where part of the original winding gear can still be seen. In 1922 Edinburgh Corporation decided to convert the entire cable system to electric traction and the number 24 tram rattled up and down North West Circus Place until the mid-1950s, when trams disappeared from Stockbridge.

Early bicycles were expensive and the large-front-wheel 'penny farthing' bicycles difficult to ride on Edinburgh's steep cobbled streets, so it was not until the 1880s when the less expensive and easier to ride 'safety bicycle' (very similar to today's models) began to become widely available that residents in the street began cycling. Alfred Nightingale, a cabinetmaker with a workshop at number 130 had a profitable sideline in buying and selling second-hand machines: 'Bicycle, safety, cushion tyres, lamp, complete, splendid condition, £6.10s.' Although Jack & Renwick at 99 St Stephen Street moved into the motor-car business by 1910, motor-cars were expensive and it was decades before many in the street could afford their own car, although they were able to travel on Edinburgh Corporation's motor buses from 1914.

Some residents, like Charles Marr who lived at number 57, began driving taxis. In 1924, only a few months after getting his licence – driving tests did not start until 1935 - he was arrested for drunk driving. The charge was not hard to prove as when he was driving along Princes Street,

1. Electric tram at bottom of Kerr
Street about to cross the bridge,
c.1930
2. Man with 'safety bicycle', c.1900
3. Edinburgh omnibus, 1926
4. Number 24 tram in Circus Place,
c. 1930s

one of the front wheels came off but, unaware or undeterred, Marr drove another 100 yards or more before stopping. When a policeman went to see what had happened, he found 'the accused hanging on to the side of his car and so drunk that he could not speak.'

The St Stephens Motor and Cycle Depot opened at 10 Henderson Row and the owner, Mr Nelson became treasurer of 'the law-abiding but dynamic new youth movement, The Road Vigilants'. The group formed in response to a local motorist deciding to go to prison rather than pay the £2 fine imposed on him for breaking the 20 mph speed limit. This was but one of many lobby groups that objected to any speed restrictions and in 1931 the government abolished them all. The adverse effect was immediate. Cyclist fatalities from motor car accidents rose from 600 a year to a peak of 1,500, and pedestrian fatalities also increased dramatically, so by 1934 the government was forced to introduce a 30mph speed limit in built-up areas, although until 1967 vehicles could travel at any speed on open roads.

1. View of North West Circus Place with cable tram, 1920
2. St Stephens Motor & Cycle Depot, Hamilton Place, c.1920s

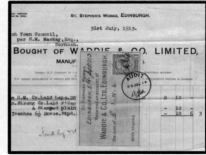

1. Printing at St Stephen's
Works, c.1930
2. Waddie & Co. paperwork,
1913
3. Office at St Stephen's Works,
c.1930
4. Waddie's delivery van,
c.1950
5. Depot for Goodyear Tyres,
c.1970s

Waddie & Co

Charles, John and Lillias Waddie, the children of a tailor in Canongate, established a stationers and lithographic printing firm in Waterloo Place in 1860. By 1874 the firm was patenting lithographic machines and requiring even larger premises, built St Stephen's Works (number 110) on an empty plot of land opposite Clarence Street. The firm printed material for a wide range of companies, including copperplate letterheads; fancy scrolls; business forms, some adorned with pictures of factories, ships and other appropriate illustrations; superfine writing papers for foreign correspondence; and antique parchment papers.

A number of its employees lived in the street and the firm's first annual social meeting for its employees in 1895 took place in St Vincent's Hall. 'Mr Charles Waddie, the managing director, presided over a crowded attendance, and an enjoyable musical programme was rendered by the employees.' Although the family firm converted into a limited liability company with a share value of £30,000 in 1890, it continued to be managed by members of the family.

Following the First World War, more opportunities arose for women to work in what earlier had been occupations reserved for men and in 1921 Rena Mitchell, who lived at number 44 was working as a compositor at St Stephen's Works. One afternoon, while on her week's holiday in St Abbs she saw a young boy who had been fishing from the rocks fall into the water. Without a second thought, Rena plunged into twenty feet of water, fully clothed, and rescued the boy. As well as being considered a heroine by her work mates, she was honoured by the Carnegie Hero Fund established in Britain in 1908 to commend bravery. 'A large company assembled in the Public Hall, St. Abbs, to honour the heroine, Miss Rena Mitchell. She was presented with a testimonial on vellum and a gold wristlet watch. After a sumptuous tea served by a willing band of ladies of the village, a short musical programme was tastefully rendered, including *Come Birdie, Home* sung by Miss A. D. Wilson. Miss Mitchell, in a neat little speech, suitably returned thanks.'

Despite extensions and improvements to St Stephen's Works over the years, the increase in business required larger premises and in 1950 the business moved to Slateford Road. In 1996 Waddie & Co was bought out from the family trusts by its management team for £16 million. In the early 1970s the building was used as a depot for Goodyear motor tyres and converted into flats in the 1980s.

HOW SCOTLAND
LOST HER PARLIAMENT

AND WHAT CAME OF IT

BY
CHARLES WADDIE

'It may chance to light on some ingredients of national feeling and set folks beards in a blaze, and so much the better if it does. I mean better for Scotland, not a whit better for me.'—*Sir Walter Scott's Journal, 21st February 1826.*

EDINBURGH: WADDIE & CO., LIMITED

1891

"BERWICK-ON-TWEED.

St Stephen's Works, Edinburgh, December 5, 1884.

SIR, - Your correspondent 'A Scotch Liberal' seems to think Berwick-on-Tweed is a Scottish town. If he inquires into the matter, however, he will find that it is an English town, under the English law, and in no way connected with Scotland but in sentiment. His reference to the Treaty of Union I don't understand. Perhaps it would be as wise to say as little on that subject as possible, as under the Treaty we are only entitled to forty-five members.

I hear so many strange references to the Treaty of Union that I rub my eyes and wonder if I have ever read that precious document. It is not a treaty that the Scots have much reason to be proud of, but it would be well for the people of Scotland if they studied it a little more, if for no other reason than that it would prevent some people from referring to a page of history they have never read.

Public opinion is slowly but surely awakening in Scotland to the fact that Scotland cannot be governed properly from London. The latest exposure of the educational muddle is opening our eyes to the ignorance, arrogance, and conceit of our Cockney rulers. May each loyal Scot earnestly pray that the rule of such blockheads may soon come to a close. - I am, &c.

THISTLEDOWN."

1. Title page of *How Scotland Lost Her Parliament*, 1891
2. Charles Waddie
3. Letter from 'Thistledown', 1884

Scottish Home Rule

In 1883 an advert appeared: 'A neat little sixpenny brochure has this week issued from the Edinburgh press of Messrs. Waddie & Co. which will no doubt be brimful of interest to many Scotsmen. It is entitled *The Treaty of Union between Scotland and England,* with an historical introduction by "Thistledown"'. Thistledown was the pen name for Charles Waddie, who owned the printing firm. Although a pro-Unionist, Charles also was a proud Scottish Nationalist and in 1886 was one of the founding members, and joint secretary, of The Scottish Home Rule Association. Its aims were: 'to maintain integrity of the empire, secure a Scottish legislature for purely Scottish matters, maintain Scotland's position within the Imperial Parliament and foster national sentiment.' Its formation was in response to William Gladstone's Irish Home Rule Bill, for Waddie and others believed that Scotland had more entitlement to Home Rule given the country's loyalty to the Crown, unlike the Irish who were being rewarded for just the opposite.

With a printing firm at his disposal, Charles published more books advocating Home Rule, as well as his own poetry and plays. His 1891 book, *How Scotland Lost Her Parliament* was welcomed by some: 'The Scotch people are beginning to discover that the union with England brought loss to this side of the border as well as some gain. An honest perusal of it can hardly fail in effecting a thorough conversion to the Home Role principle'. Yet many others were scathing of those who supported Home Rule for Scotland, calling them 'eccentric fanatics.' In 1893 Charles wrote to the Prince of Wales complaining about a lecture delivered by William Lecky (an Irish historian) at which the Prince had presided. 'Mr Lecky spoke of the British Empire as the sole possession of England and entirely ignored the fact that Scotland has contributed far out of proportion to her population to the building up of the Empire.'

For a time it appeared that the campaign for Home Rule would succeed. Between 1886 and 1900 Scottish Home Rule was debated seven times at Westminster, and in 1895 the Commons voted in favour of a resolution for Home Rule, but it ran out of Parliamentary time. In the year before his death in 1912, Charles despaired: 'I feel a sinking of the heart when I consider that I have spent some of the best years of a long life trying to rouse you [the Scottish nation] from your present apathy.' The year after Charles died it appeared that his longed-for vision of Scotland would be realised as the House of Commons voted 204 to 159 to bring in federalisation for Scotland. However, the First World War prevented the bill from progressing and Scotland had to wait until 1999 for its own Parliament.

PRISON AT 76 YEARS OF AGE.—At Edinburgh
Burgh Court yesterday forenoon Bailie Brown
passed sentence of two months' imprisonment on an
old woman, Maria M'Queen, 76 years of age, who
was stated to reside in lodgings at 49 St Stephen
Street, Edinburgh. There were four charges of
theft against the woman, who pleaded guilty to
having stolen, from four shops, a table cloth,
two pairs of stockings, a pair of gloves, and a
chemise. She had had six previous convictions,
the last in 1898. It was stated that the woman
had no friends or relatives in the city, and the
Magistrate remarked that he found it a difficult
case to deal with, but thought that prison was
the best course. As she was led down the stairs
from the Court the woman halted and pleaded to
be sent to a home.

1. Fire Station and Police Station in Hamilton Place, c.1900
2. Court report, 1929
3. Edinburgh Constable, c.1870

Crime

The street has had its fair share of crime in spite of harsh penalties. In 1828 William Johnston was found guilty of 'entering the premises of Messrs. Carson and Broom, Brunswick Street, and carrying off goods to the value of £10,14s, and being of habit and repute' was sentenced to 14 years transportation.

Much of the crime was shoplifting or petty theft, arising from poverty. As today, life for many artists was hand-to-mouth and in 1902, with the festive pantomime season at an end, Abe Gilbert, a comedian lodging in the street, stole a lady's chatelaine bag and two watches from a stationer's shop in Princes Street. The watches were pawned and the lady's bag presented to an actress he admired. Rather than 14 years in Australia, Gilbert was sentenced to 14 days in the city's jail.

In the late 1840s Stockbridge Police Station was opened at 5 Hamilton Place and, a decade or so later, a fire station was built next to it at number 3. As Brunswick Street was close by, policemen often lived in the street, including Constable Donald Swanston at number 31 in 1865 and Sergeant Andrew Mackenzie at number 16 in 1906. Around 1910 the police and fire stations in Hamilton Place closed and moved to new buildings in Saunders Street. The old police station building was used by the City Council as a store and then in 1935 converted by the Scottish Wayfarers Welfare Society into a hostel for young homeless men. That had to close in 1939, as it was taken over to store equipment for air raid wardens. In recent years it has housed a restaurant, while the old fire station became public toilets.

Violent incidents were not uncommon, more often than not fuelled by alcohol. The regular court appearances of husbands in the street charged with assaulting their wives indicates that domestic violence was widespread, and often not taken very seriously. In 1879 David Greig, who assaulted his wife, only received a £2 cautionary bond against 'future good behaviour' rather than a fine or imprisonment whereas three years earlier when, unusually, Mrs Cox was found guilty of striking her husband's arm with a poker, she was sentenced to 20 days imprisonment. No doubt the more severe sentence was due to Mr Cox having told the court his wife drank heavily as the hypocritical view of the time was that female drunkenness was beyond the pale, while men drinking heavily was accepted.

On two occasions wives living in the street were murdered by their husbands. The most recent was in 1998 when Margaret Reid, a mother of five, was discovered in a skip in Henderson Place Lane, having been violently assaulted and stabbed. Her apparently distraught husband reported her missing some days before the body was discovered and for a time the police sought a mystery killer. However, Reid finally was arrested

TRAFFICKING VICE SCANDAL

Before Bailie Gibson, in Edinburgh City Police Court to-day, Simeon Arkend (42), Russian Jew, described as a shoemaker, living at St Stephen Street, was convicted of creating a disturbance in his house and the stair in the early hours of yesterday morning, shouting and bawling, and quarrelling with the woman with whom he cohabited, to the annoyance of the neighbours. The case disclosed another of many similar instances that frequently transpire in the police court of young women in Edinburgh who have come under the baneful influence of foreigners, mostly Polish Jews, who in addition to making their unfortunate victims their breadwinners, while they themselves live a life of ease and idleness, systematically ill-treat them. Arkend was sent to prison for 60 day. The sentence was received with applause in court.

1. Mrs Margaret Reid, c.1990s
2. Newspaper article about murder in St Stephen Street of Elizabeth Smith by her husband William Smith, 1953
3. Edinburgh Constable, c.1970s
4. Newspaper article, 1902

and it transpired that he had killed Margaret because she told him she planned to leave him, hid the body in an underground recess to the kitchen and a few nights later transferred Margaret's body to Henderson Place Lane. He was sentenced to life imprisonment.

In 1876 Mary Ann McKenna who lived in Market Place was fined for a 'disturbance in her house that does not bear a spotless reputation', this being the newspaper's discreet description of a house of ill-repute. McKenna was not the only prostitute to live in the street and no doubt almost all were coerced into prostitution by men. The role of men as pimps was seldom mentioned in court reports, except when a foreigner was involved, and then often with a racist, or as in this 1902 instance, an anti-Semitic overtone. Simeon Arkend, a forty-two-year-old Russian Jew living in St Stephen Street was arrested when neighbours complained that he was shouting and quarrelling with the woman with whom he cohabited. 'The case disclosed another of many similar instances that frequently transpire in the police court of young women in Edinburgh who have come under the baneful influence of foreigners, mostly Polish Jews, who in addition to making their unfortunate victims their breadwinners, while they themselves live a life of ease and idleness, systematically ill-treat them. The judge's sentence on Arkend of 60 days was received with applause in court.'

Gambling in Britain was made illegal from the mid-nineteenth century and in 1906 the Street Betting Act further criminalised all gambling, except for betting at racecourses. This stemmed partly from a view that it was immoral for the working class to gamble, while the same was not thought true of the wealthy who attended horse racing. Of course gambling did bring hardship; many children have gone without food when their father's (or less often mother's) certain winner flopped. However, the ban on off-course betting was pointless as gambling remained rife among all communities. Instead illegal street runners took bets on behalf of undercover bookies. Andrew Foley at number 32 was a street bookie and he was caught and fined, although it is likely he was back on the street within a day or two, perhaps even taking a sly bet from an off-duty policeman. The street also had basements where people played cards for money and in 1934 Margaret Allen was fined for the second time for having an illegal gambling machine in her shop at number 122.

By the early 1990s it was theft from cars and vandalism that featured prominently in the Stockbridge & New Town independent newsletter.

1. Stockbridge Duck race, 2010 (photo -
Richard Findlay)
2. Scott Hutchison performing at Record
Day concert in St Stephen Place organised
by Darren of VoxBox Music, 2017 (photo -
Instagram)
3. Stockbridge Festival Programme, 1991
4. Colourful crowd at the 1991 Festival
(photo - Peter Stubbs)

Community Events

The revival in St Stephen Street's fortunes has been part of a wider regeneration in Stockbridge and local entrepreneurial spirit, and has led to a number of community events.

In 1988 Susie Gregor , a local resident, saw a duck race and decided that the Water of Leith was the perfect place for a similar event. So in that year the Stockbridge Duck Race was launched when hundreds of intrepid yellow plastic ducks plunged into the river, racing to be first to reach Falshaw Bridge. Over its thirty plus years the annual event has grown to become a huge community event. Support from local businesses donating prizes and selling tickets has raised tens of thousands of pounds for charity over the years. On the day of the race the plastic ducks are released into the Water of Leith at 3pm from the bridge beside Pizza Express and the resolute ducks then race down to Falshaw Bridge. Along the course the ducks are marshalled by volunteer "Duck Wardens" to ensure that every duck makes it to the finishing line. Numbers are called out at the finish line and winners receive their prizes. Traditionally, the event is followed by an evening 'Apres Duck' party in St Stephen Street hosted by either The Bailie or The Antiquary with entertainment.

Throughout the 1990s there was a Stockbridge Festival that ran for a week in the summer with concerts, exhibitions, poetry readings and other events taking place at venues throughout the area. The first in 1991 included a concert in St Stephen's Church featuring the renowned violinist, Leonard Friedman.

In 2012 Darren Yeats who ran VoxBox Music at number 21 decided to participate in the UK's Record Store Day by organising live music in the street. After a series of successful annual events he decided to move the 2019 event indoors and St Vincent's Chapel agreed to house it. However, running any such event is far from straightforward as Darren recounted: 'The Council called the Rector of St Vincent's, threatening to shut all of the future church events down if they allow us in for Record Store Day. It will be chaos they said, they don't have the permissions!' He had but this did not stop the Chapel's events man coming to the record store to ask again. 'He arrived at the shop. Record boxes were covering the floor as a late delivery had just come in and 240 cans of Innis and Gunn lager had also arrived.'

In the end all was resolved and the event went ahead with a series of acts performing to an appreciative crowd. Darren recounts that at the end the event he met a retired clergywoman in the makeshift bar area. '"Jesus would have loved this" she said. He loved a party!" And that is basically what I will put on the Licence application for next year.'

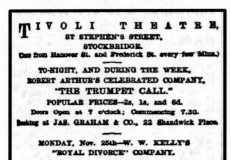

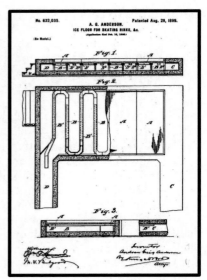

1, Advert for Eckersley & Laverick, St Stephen's Engine Works, 1876
2. Drawing as part of Andrew Anderson's Patent for his ice floor for skating rinks, 1899
3. Advert for Tivoli Theatre, 1902
4. George White's Novelty Switchback ride, 1900

Entertainment at number 99

Until 1899 the area of ground between the solitary house on the corner of Clarence Street and St Stephen's Church contained various businesses. In 1869 Quigley & Co Printers moved into a workshop there, bringing in heavy equipment including letter presses, a steam engine and racks of lead type, but within months the firm had gone into sequestration and the whole lot was advertised for auction. The premises were taken over by Eckersley & Laverick, a firm of engineers and machinists. Other firms in the area included a cabinetmaker, and John Dawson's firm of bell hangers and makers of Venetian blinds.

In the late 1890s the land was purchased by Andrew Grieg Anderson, the owner of John Anderson & Sons, fishmongers, poulterers and game dealers that traded from the Royal Emporium, Castle Street. As the firm also sold ice, Anderson had a keen interest in its production and storage, and in 1899 he successfully applied to the American Patent Office for: 'new and useful improvements in or relating to Ice Floors for Skating-Rinks and in the Manufacture of Ice, also applicable for cooling and purifying air in dairies, hospitals, and other similar buildings and places.' On the site he first erected an ice storage facility and then commissioned the architect. Thomas Marwick and the builder, Colin Macandrew to erect a large building to house a skating rink to show off his invention.

Although the building was completed by 1899, the ice-skating rink was never installed. Instead, an advert appeared in November 1900 offering the building for sale: 'Large hall, measuring 190 feet long by 79 feet wide and about 45 feet high. The roof is in one span without pillars. There is also an annex measuring 60 by 50 feet, divided into several apartments. The hall is fitted up with electric light and is admirably suited for a skating rink, drill hall, circus, hippodrome, concerts, cycling exhibitions or theatrical performances.'

No buyers came forward so Anderson leased the building to George White. He operated fun-fair rides around Scotland and for three months the building, was named The Hippodrome and housed a fun fair with 'a switchback ride.'

The building then was leased and converted into the Tivoli Theatre by Weldon Watts, an English theatre owner. The Tivoli opened in November 1901: 'Watts slated a popular piece for the set-off, and the furious fun of "Swiss Express" kept up almost a continuous flow of merriment. The theatre itself is a commodious and comfortable building, plainly but yet tastefully decorated. There is sitting accommodation for about 2,000 persons. The lighting is by electricity, and the same motive power is used to drive the ventilating fans in the roof. As a precaution against fire, a pipe has been placed along the top of the front of the stage, from which a

1. Eade Montefiore in his office, 1905
2. Eddie Gifford, the trick cyclist, c.1904
3. A Postcard advertising the opening production at the Grand Theatre, with Miss May Marton as Cinderella, Miss Millie Engler as Prince Rupert, and Little Zola as Buttons. Caption Reads 'Buttons: "That's your little game! I'll call again tomorrow.", 1904
4. Osmond Tearle as Coriolanus

continuous downpour of water can be brought, entirely isolating the stage from the auditorium. The whole theatre is heated on the hot-water system.'

The shows presented at The Tivoli were diverse. In March 1902 the Osmond Tearle Shakespearian Company performed a different Shakespeare play each evening for a week, but mostly the theatre presented evenings of variety: 'The principal attraction at the Tivoli Theatre this week is a party of six lady international wrestlers. The company includes the lady wrestler, Miss Bradford from Liverpool, who offers £10 to any lady she fails to throw in 15 minutes. The entertainment may not be edifying nor graceful, but is novel. The programme concludes with an exhibition of animated pictures depicting scenes at Hampton Park races.' In December Eddie Gifford, a trick cyclist, was the star attraction. 'After giving a clever trick-riding display, Gifford and his machine are hauled up by rope to the roof of the theatre, where an opening has been cut out the boards and a small stage erected. Thirty feet below, in the orchestra stalls area, a space about 15 feet square has been cleared and occupied by a large tank of water, about 15 feet deep. Gifford cycles to the edge of the stage above and, on the bicycle on which he is seated, drops into the tank. The daring of the feat is enhanced by the fact that Gifford possesses but one leg.' One dares not imagine what stunts this encouraged young Stockbridge dare-devil cyclists to attempt!

After just two years Watts gave up and John McArthur, who operated a number of theatres around Scotland, became the lessee. He renamed it The Grand and appointed Eade Montefiore as its manager. In November 1904 an advert appeared in the Edinburgh Evening News: 'Grand Theatre, Edinburgh. Wanted 50 ladies to go in the pantomime, Cinderella. Those who can sing and dance are advised to write, in the first instance, to Mr Eade Montefiore.' Perhaps at least one young woman living in St Stephen Street successfully applied and had the thrill of performing in front of her family and neighbours. 'The Grand opens its doors to the public to-night. Everything possible has been done to ensure the comfort of the audience and Mr Montefiore, who is something of a connoisseur in art, has adorned the walls of the promenade, the smoking-room, and the ladies' room with a very fine collection of engravings, which include about 150 examples of Hogarth's best-known works.'

Although one doubts whether they took part in the actual game, many of the fifty ladies starring in the pantomime would have attended Heart of Midlothian's Football Club's ground to watch a Grand Theatre Pantomime Eleven play the Hotel Employees' Register and Club in a match to raise funds for the Evening News charity fund. 'Kick-off 5.30 by The Prince - Miss Florrie Forde. Kick-Off at Half-Time by Miss Gertie Gitana.' Although it was reported that the Hotel Employees won by four

1. The building, c.1970s
2. Advert for Grand Theatre, 1905
3. Advert for Jack and Renwick, 1910
4. Napier Landaulette Motor Car, 1911

goals to two, there were boos from the Pantomime players who were convinced the real score was four goals to three in their favour.

The next production was somewhat different: 'From the frivolity of the pantomime to *Uncle Tom's Cabin* in which the elements of tragedy, pathos, and humour, are mixed, is a great change, and there was a large house at the Grand Theatre last night to welcome the production of the play based on Mrs Beecher Stowe's great work. A touch of realism is given by the employment of several Negroes and the play keeps strictly to the beaten track.' In 1905 early films and pseudo-scientific displays began to be shown as part of the theatrical programmes: 'Dr Walford Bodie, an exponent of electro-therapeutics, last night gave an electrical demonstration between the variety acts, and professed to have effected some astounding cures. Helpless little children were carried on, and after undergoing treatment, threw aside their surgical boots, and, using their shrunk and withered limbs, went off smiling and unaided. These were said to be cases of paralysis which, by local medical institutions had been pronounced hopeless and incurable.' One wonders how much local children were paid to act the part of 'the cripples'. However, John McArthur's attempts to make the building work as a theatre also failed, so in the autumn of 1906 the Grand Theatre closed and its contents were auctioned off, including 'over two hundred old and modern engravings and prints'; presumably including those by Hogarth.

In 1907 The New York Animated Picture Company took the tenancy and showed early films. 'The ingenious *Liquid Electricity* struck quite an unusual vein, and caused great merriment.' This early film showed a mad scientist figuring out how to convert electricity to a liquid and then spraying it on slow moving people, whereupon they moved like lightning. The film simply was the gag repeated four or five times. Within months that use ended and Lyon & Turnbull auctioned off the remaining theatre fittings, including hundreds of tip-up seats, curtains, and the innovative electric ventilator fans and iron water sprinkler.

The large, now empty, building was leased by James Jack and Peter Renwick in the summer of 1908. They were horse dealers and jobmasters - men who rented out horses and carriages by the job – and advertised under two titles: the Edinburgh Riding Academy and the Edinburgh Horse Repository. The Riding Academy offered evening classes in horse handling. 'An interesting display of mounted sports was given last night in the Riding Academy by the D Squadron of the Lothians and Border Horse. The items embraced a Balaclava melee, bareback wrestling and pushball. The manner in which both men and horses went through various manoeuvres indicated careful training.' Jack & Renwick held a weekly auction of horses, carriages and harnesses and at their first auction over 100 horses were put up for sale. Jack & Renwick then began to move into

94

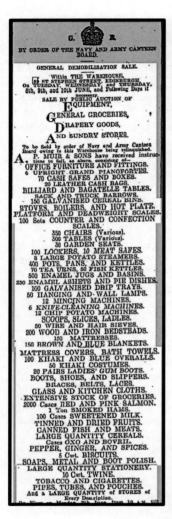

1. Sale of First World War surplus equipment, 1919
2. *Across India with H.R.H. the Duke of Connaught* film, 1921
3. Advert for Charlie Chaplin's *The Gold Rush*, July 1926
4. Advert for film showings at The Grand including *Yes we have no Bonanzas*, 1939

the motor-car business and were one of the first in the city to advertise motor cars for hire. 'Shopping and Town calling in luxurious Landaulettes (open-topped models) at very low rates'. In 1917 Jack & Renwick moved to premises in Bells Brae in Dean Village.

From early 1918 the premises were used by the Navy and Army Canteen Board to store equipment that was required in the First World War and in June 1919 was the site for a huge auction of equipment no longer required, including ladies gum boots, chip potato machines, tea urns and even billiard tables.

On 31 December 1920 the building opened as the Grand Picture House seating 1,600 people. In July 1921 the cinema hosted a private view of the first ever film of a Royal Indian Tour - *Across India with H.R.H. the Duke of Connaught* and the audience included a number of Indian students from Edinburgh University. Through the 1920s and early 1930s the Grand was one of the city's cinemas that gave an annual showing for disadvantaged children, organised by the Edinburgh Courant newspaper: 'Ten thousand poor children in Edinburgh were the guests yesterday of the Courant Fund at various cinema entertainments in the city. Each child on leaving the entertainment received a bag of cakes and fruit, which fittingly rounded off an enjoyable treat'. By 1930, with the advent of commercial films with fully synchronised sound, the Grand was advertising itself as a 'Super Talkie House'.

Pressure from the church, and even within the cinema trade, meant that it was not until after the Second World War that cinemas in Edinburgh were licensed to show films on Sundays. In 1931 Mr Albin, president of the East of Scotland section of the Cinema Exhibitors' Association said: 'I don't think that a regular Sunday night performance would justify itself financially in a city of Edinburgh's size. It would only take people off Saturday night.' The only exception was charity film shows on Sundays in one month each year.

By a strange coincidence, on 3 September 1939, when Britain declared war on Germany, one of the films showing at the Grand was *Yes we have no Bonanzas* – a parody of the 1923 song *Yes! We Have No Bananas* – starring The Three Stooges, an American comedy team. In the war the British government banned imports of bananas for five years and greengrocers in Stockbridge no doubt were among the many shops that posted signs in their windows stating 'Yes, we have no bananas' in keeping with the war spirit. One woman recalled going to the Grand just after the war when still a youngster: 'In the 50's we had to take bottled 'sugar ally water' (water with a hard liquorice stick left in it for a few days to give it flavour) instead of juice because of rationing. Sometimes we had to leave without seeing the end of the film as there were many power cuts after the war.' Another recalls it being cheap but 'a flea pit'.

1. Poster for Frankie Miller Band at Tiffanys, 1976
2. Bingo session, early 1960s
3. Little Richard
4. Advert for Little Richard at the Pentland Club, 1966
5. Complimentary book of matches advertising Cinderellas Rockerfellas, 1980s
6. Entrance to Tiffanys, 1970s

In 1960 the Betting and Gaming Act legalised commercial bingo and like many cinemas, the films at the Grand were replaced by calls of 'Legs eleven' and 'A monkey's cousin' as it became the Grand Bingo Hall. By 1963 more than 14 million people had become members of commercial bingo clubs around the UK, and like other such clubs, the Grand Bingo Hall served as a meeting place and social hub for the community. However, the media resorted to moralisation, condescension and in some cases outright vilification of bingo. The Times derided the game as a 'cretinous pastime', denouncing female players who (allegedly) sent their children 'after a hasty tea to hold their mother's places in the queue'.

The bingo club closed in 1966 and Ray Grehan, who ran a number of music clubs in North East England and managed a number of musical acts, opened the Pentland Club in the building. It hosted national and international acts including, in December 1966, the flamboyant US rock & roll star, Little Richard for ten nights. Given his stage persona involved a pompadour hairstyle, androgynous makeup and glitzy clothes, one wonders what the New Town's then conservative residents would have thought if they had glimpsed the outrageous, flamboyantly dressed, gay American strolling through their sombre city streets.

The club changed its name to Tiffanys in the early 1970s and featured punk, reggae and new-wave music, including Iggy Pop, Elvis Costello and Aswad. By 1980 it hosted acts such as Simple Minds, Siouxsie & The Banshees and the Police. One club-goer recalled her evenings there: 'I went to quite a few gigs at the old dive that was Tiffanys in Stockbridge. God those fishing nets and glass balls hanging from the ceiling! The best act by far was The Pretenders. Chrissie and the boys put on a great show. When the crowd roared for more she said "Sorry but we've played everything we know!" They were supported by a then unheard of UB40!'

Later in the 1970s George Duffin, who ran the Cosmos music agency, noticed that the venue was always shut on Mondays so negotiated with its then manager Ken Smith a rent-free deal for Monday evenings. Smith doubted anyone would go but was proved spectacularly wrong as Tiffanys became the best attended Monday night gig in the UK, part of its appeal being that it was the only city venue with a Monday late drinks licence. Mondays at Tiffanys provided starts for many fledgling Edinburgh bands. As ticket agencies did not exist, tickets were sold around the pubs by young women who received one free ticket for every nine sold,

Around 1980 it was renamed Cinderella Rockerfellas and continued as a music venue and discotheque. One of the disk jockeys was John Leslie, who later found fame as a presenter of the children's TV programme, *Blue Peter*. However, in May 1991 the building burned down, bringing to an end its colourful ninety years, and the site was redeveloped as flats.

1. Edinburgh dairy milk can, c.1850s
2. Advert for hosier and glover at 8 Baker's Place, 1840
3. Boot & shoe repairer window, 1910
4. Advert for butcher at number 41 , 1877
5. Advert for music shop at number 9, 1900

The street's shops

Today's small shops house a diversity of flourishing business that draw people from far and wide, yet for most of its 200 years they were local affairs, selling necessities for nearby residents : grocers, bakers, hairdressers, butchers, greengrocers, dairies, shoemakers, leather-workers, etc. There also were dressmakers, tailors, bonnet-makers and others who worked from small workshops or a room in their flat. Three of the earliest with work premises in the street were James Luke, a baker; George Hewat, a wine and spirit merchant; and Charles Dunlop, a cabinetmaker.

Like most dairies in the 19th century, those in the street supplied fresh milk from cows kept nearby and the dairy owners were often termed 'cowfeeders' or 'cowkeepers'. Many of the cows that provided the milk sold in the street were kept in the nearby Silvermills area, in spite of cowsheds in populated areas being a significant health risk. In 1888 William Wilson, who had a small dairy in the street, pleaded guilty for having: 'failed to keep his cow-house or byre, situated at Silvermills, in a thoroughly clean and wholesome condition.' The city worked to close down such cowsheds but even by 1900 there were still 115 licensed cowsheds in the city, containing around 3,000 cows.

Adverts for shops in the street began to appear in the 1850s, although these were few: shop-keepers whose trade was local would not have needed to advertise and others could not afford the cost. James Weddell, a wine merchant, was an early advertiser although his advert was notifying customers that his business temporarily had moved to Brunswick Street from Bakers' Place (Kerr Street) due to 'the total destruction of the stock and premises by fire. We trust that any inconvenience arising from this arrangement will, in the circumstances, be overlooked.' Most of those who advertised were small businesses promoting their wares to the more prosperous parts of the New Town: 'William Hannah, surgeon and dentist – enabled to sell the best Artificial Teeth.' 'Straw and felt hat cleaner and dyer. Hats and bonnets altered. G. W. Dunham, 6 Brunswick Street.' 'Evening parties attended to with the violin. Dance music. Terms moderate. J. Robertson, 14 Brunswick Street.' D. Willoughby, who was employed by Edinburgh Academy to teach and play cricket at the school, opened a shop in Market Place where he sold: 'seasoned cricket bats, Lillywhite Guide to Cricketers, scoring sheets and every article connected with the noble game.' One of the earliest mentions of an eatery appeared in 1883: 'Dining and refreshment room, 41 Brunswick Street. Fish and Tripe suppers'.

Shops selling second-hand goods began to open. Fraser Campbell, who had trained as an upholsterer, bought and sold used furniture, and musical

1. Advert for cricket shop at number 8 Market Place, 1864
2. Advert for bird shop at number 26, 1881
3. Advert for basket and brush shop at numbers 8 and 10, 1878
4. McPherson Confectioners, at numbers 118 & 120 1917

101

instruments: 'Square piano 45s; magnificent square 5 guineas; splendid harmonium 70s; violin and bow 25s; double bass, 4 strings only 4 guineas.' Another second-hand 'apparel' dealer, Mr Houston at number 12, advertised to buy a diversity of items, including, 'old artificial teeth'.

It is likely that some residents would have raised and raced pigeons, while there was a fashion for keeping singing birds in cages, and so Henry King opened a shop in the street selling: 'all kinds of fancy Scotch canaries for breeding purposes; also linnets, Larks and all kinds of pigeons.' Occasionally horses were advertised for sale or to purchase, although C. Loppens' advertisement is somewhat chilling: 'old horses to kill; good prices given.'

Over the decades shops must have had to deal with many irate customers, but an incident from 1902 must surely be unique. Ann Mason, a twenty-four-year old fish hawker, went into Ferguson's fish shop at number 13 to purchase herrings. When the shop assistant handed them over, Mason became angry, complaining that the herrings were substandard and: 'lifting a large cod fish from off the shelf, struck the shop girl with it.' The court hearing at which Mason was fined 10s 6d was reported in the press under the heading: 'A cod as a weapon.' Sadly, nothing has been traced for the splendidly named Garden Burnett, an illusionist and ventriloquist, who lived at number 5 and advertised: 'No entertainment is complete without Burnett, the Premier: A Vision or Illusory Entertainment; on tour with own show.'

By the 1930s the street's shops were in decline. In 1934 the Edinburgh Evening News ran a special advertising feature: 'Stockbridge – A shopping centre' but the only shop advertised in St Stephen Street was a second-hand furniture warehouse. Few adverts for businesses in the street appeared except regular announcements of sales of unredeemed goods from the pawnbroker at number 10. Many businesses came and went within a few years. One exception was James Anderson's hairdressers at number 24, which opened around 1920; even though James died in 1950, the shop continued through to at least the 1970s. By 1960 many shops in the street were vacant and a number of those in basements unusable. By the end of the decade, however, there was a dramatic change in the street's fortunes, thanks to the youth-driven cultural revolution that had emerged in London - the 'Swinging Sixties' - for even straight-laced, Presbyterian Edinburgh was not immune to this Bohemian impulse. As one person who lived in St Stephen Street joked: 'In the 70s overnight all the second hand shops became antique shops.'

The city's 1973 report into the street's future identified the change in more official language: 'St Stephen Street contains many small specialist shops which bear no direct relationship to the shopping in the rest of the area. These specialist shops have grown up due to the availability of low

1. Advert for Stephen Brickman at number 28, 1953
2. Confectioner's shop at number 51, 1900 (thanks to Garry McGravie)
3. Antique shop at number 13, 1980
4. Moondance at number 18, 1971
5. The Astrology Centre at number 60, c.1990

rateable value property which has enabled small shops to start with a low capital investment. In some cases the traders display their wares on the stairs in front of their shops.'

One of those who took advantage of the low rents was Lizzie MacDonald, who opened her shop in 1970. At this time there was a long-running coal miner's strike that brought electricity cuts to the nation. For significant periods, homes and businesses had to go without power and candles were much in demand. Lizzie spotted a business opportunity. 'I had practically no money but had learned to make sand candles that were cast using very hot wax poured into bowl-shaped impressions into damp sand. The resulting candles burnt for days - not hours. In those days, it was hard for shop landlords to even find tenants at five pounds a week. I approached the owner and convinced him to let me have the shop for rent to be paid in arrears. The shop had a stove and I set to work. My first big customer was The Scotsman office wanting candles for reporters to type by. I also placed a notice in my shop window inviting local crafts people to sell their work through my shop on commission. I named it Moondance after Van Morrison's song and painted the steps in an American flag so customers could walk/trample on it. I sold it 18 months later to travel.'

By 1983, alongside the street's half-a-dozen antique shops, shoppers could buy Latin American folk art at Azteca (number 12); fashionable second-hand clothes at Old Habits Die Hard (53); macrobiotic foods at East West Centre (12); designer clothes at Tommy Rot (60); and even learn their fortune at the Astrology Centre (60). Those who are part of today's resurgence of interest in LPs would have had a field day at the Gramophone Emporium (21): 'Most large cities have one or two shops that have some sort of 78rpm speciality – in Edinburgh, the Gramophone Emporium in St Stephens Street is a treasure-house.'

Shops in the street began to feature in up-market magazines; such as Montresor that opened at number 35 in 1993:'This is an Aladdin's Cave of twinkling trinkets. Its old curiosity shop interior drips with glittering glass gems exquisitely set in paste and plastic treasures unearthed from attics, antique shops and auctions, which until recently would have been looked upon by many with disdain.'

Bell's Diner brought American-style burgers to the street fifty years ago in 1972 and by 1990 had been joined by other world cuisines including: French - Ma Cuisine; Chinese - Unicorn Inn; Malaysian - Teh's Kitchen; Mexican - Blue Parrot; and Peruvian - Café Pena Jaranti.

The street continues to attract notable shops. In 2012 Mark Jones, a former director of the National Museums of Scotland and London's Victoria & Albert Museum, opened Golden Hare Books at number 68, and in 2020 Larah Bross opened another of her successful bagel shops next door.

THE BAILIE

NOW TAKING BOOKINGS
FOR CHRISTMAS LUNCH PARTIES

TRADITIONAL MENU AVAILABLE

QUALITY SELECTION OF REAL ALES
THEAKSTONS - IPA - DIRECTORS - FLOWERS

ATMOSPHERE SECOND TO NONE

ARE YOU PARTY HATS & CRACKERS?

THE BAILIE
2 ST. STEPHEN STREET
STOCKBRIDGE
EDINBURGH
TEL: (0131) 225 4673

IMPORTANT TO THE PUBLIC.

ALE made upon an improved principle, and possessing qualities highly recommendatory.

The lovers of this most healthy beverage may be supplied by the Subscribers, with such a fine quality as very seldom has, if ever before, been submitted to the public.

That the greater proportion of Ale which is manufactured is of a soft worty consistency, changeable it its character by a slight change of temperature, and that such can neither be wholesome or palatable will readily be admitted.

The desideratum is, therefore, to produce such a quality, as will not only be light on the palate, but possessing such a firmness of body as will maintain its purity, even by exposure to a great change of temperature.

The Subscribers, after a great many trials and experiments made to produce a liquor of the character now alluded to, and so generally inquired after, have much satisfaction in acquainting the Public, that from Brewings they have had, and the test which has been made, they have every confidence in thinking their labours have been successful.

The Ale now submitted is exclusively made for the sale of the Subscribers (sealed with green wax and G. H. stamped X.X.X.), and from its highly attenuated character, is beautifully transparent, of fine flavour, and & Co. possesses all the saccharine richness which the finest malt is capable of producing.

The Subscribers have also to recommend their extensive Stock of WINES of all kinds, in full state of maturity. Foreign and British SPIRITS, LIQUEURS, and COMPOUNDS, all selected from the first houses at home and abroad.

George Street Wine Vaults, No. 35,
and No. 1, Brunswick Street.
GEO. HEWAT & CO.

1. View of the bar before it was named
The Bailie and missing its entrance
lantern, 1971
2. The Bailie lantern
3. Advert for Christmas lunch, c.1990
4. Advert for George Hewat's ale, 1834

The Bailie

The Bailie Bar at 2-4 St Stephen Street has been serving people drinks since 1825. That year George Hewat, a wine and spirit merchant in George Street took the basement premises and ran it until his retirement in 1847. He sold the premises to Robert Dickson who lived at number 19. It is unlikely that Dickson had much time for his neighbour at number 38, Ebeneezer Murray for he was President of the Edinburgh Total Abstinence Society, and in 1853 the powerful temperance lobby reduced pub closing times to 11pm and introduced complete closure on Sundays. .

Before electric lighting, the three rooms would have been murky. William Fraser who had the premises in the early 1880s was found guilty of 'supplying liquor to a person who was intoxicated' and fined. In spite of this being his only conviction, the police objected to his licence being renewed. Fraser pleaded that he had borrowed money to buy the goodwill and fittings, and he needed to continue as his recent business had been poor as 'the property is not the best place for a bar being dark and downstairs.' He was allowed to keep his licence.

By 1897 the bar was owned by Robert Stirling and when he applied to take on the licence, Bailie Mackenzie suggested that the introduction of electric light would greatly improve the premises and Stirling agreed to do so, spending around £500 on lighting and internal improvements. It may have been at this point that women were allowed to drink in a separate area, although there were no female toilets for decades. As the Grand Theatre in St Stephen Street did not have a drinks licence, Stirling's bar did good business in the intervals of the shows and probably it is then that the bar became known as the 'Grand Bar'.

In 1907 Stirling left and the bar was bought by Charles Henry Dundas Ross and John Alexander Ross; the latter having been working as a chemist's assistant before taking on running the bar.

The temperance movement continued to be strong and its campaigning led to the introduction of the Temperance (Scotland) Act 1913, which enabled voters in local areas to decide whether their area should remain 'wet' or go 'dry'. At a meeting of 1,300 local electors in the Grand Cinema, perhaps attracted by the free musical programme rather than the various speeches, St Stephen's Ward voted to remain 'wet' by 3,626 votes to 1,266.

In 1971 the Grand Bar was bought by Hamish Henderson who before becoming an owner of various bars had worked as a theatre designer, including with the Royal Lyceum Theatre in its first season. He renamed it The Bailie after a theatre production, and during the early 1980s expanded the premises into the adjoining two basement properties.

Stockbridge Market

1. Front entrance to Stockbridge Market, c.1900
2. Advert for New Town Market, 1824
3. Drawing of part of Stockbridge Market by Robert Diaz, 1892
4. Advert, 1879

Stockbridge Market

In 1824, Captain David Carnegie launched a proposal for a new meat, fish, vegetable and fruit market. Carnegie was born in Leith and served with the 44th Infantry during the Peninsula War. After the defeat of Napoleon in 1815 he resigned from the army and returned to Scotland, establishing a wine merchant business in Duke Street, Leith. He was married to Mary de la Condamine, the daughter of the King's Advocate General of Guernsey.

To part-finance the scheme he sold shares in the New Town Markets Company, although he remained part proprietor and acted as manager of the project. At the company's annual meeting shareholders were informed: 'A site for the establishment of a subdivision market in the north-east quarter of the city has already been secured. A more eligible site for the erection of markets could not have been found within the four corners of the city.'

Carnegie commissioned Archibald Scott, a young architect, to create a building on the model of Liverpool market. The grand entrance in Market Place (now St Stephens Place) has survived, although the rest of the building is long gone. The market opened in April 1826: 'On Saturday last, the splendid New Town markets at Brunswick Street were opened, and visited by thousands of the citizens, who crowded to them from an early hour in the morning. When we look not only to the comfort and cleanliness everywhere displayed in these markets, but to the extreme elegance of their structure and reflect that they have been projected and executed at the sole expense and risk of patriotic citizens, we cannot omit this opportunity of expressing our high opinion of Captain Carnegie's public spirited exertions.'

Then followed a detailed description: 'The markets occupy a quadrangle comprising nearly an acre and a half. On the southern side one enters from Brunswick Street and the entrance is adorned with two handsome columns while the northern gate opens into the road to Silvermills. The quadrangle is divided by a solid stone wall and a gate divides the two and can be closed when necessary. The smaller northern part is exclusively for the sale of fish, while the larger quadrangle is for flesh, poultry, vegetables, fruit, &c. The separation of the fish from the flesh in this way is by no means a useless refinement when it is considered that fish have naturally a strong odour, and that the sense of smell is of so much use in marketing, that it ought to be as little disturbed as possible by extrinsic effluvia. The large quadrangle consists, first, of one long straight avenue from the gate to the gate at the Brunswick Street end, which is covered in from end to end, and lighted from the roof and has a row of stalls on each side. The second avenue also has a double row of stalls, one on your right hand and the other on your left. This avenue is open in the middle for the sake of

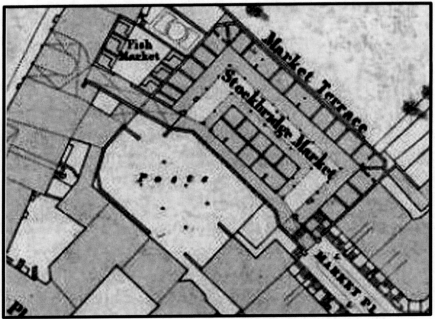

1. Hamilton Place entrance to Stockbridge Market, c.1910
2. Market layout, detail from 1851 map by Robert Kirkwood (National Library of Scotland)
(opposite page) Advert for sale of the market, 1895

better ventilation and has a covered portico. On the second floor there is a single row of stalls all round the exterior wall. All the area is flagged. The passage from the lower to the upper area is by two broad stairs. The roofs of the galleries are supported by slender fluted columns of cast iron, and the open side of the upper gallery is guarded by an ornamental iron rail. The front of the stalls or shops is formed of trellis work, painted green and designed in a very neat style. The whole is planned and executed with great taste, and has the commodious and elegance we would expect to find in a Fancy Bazaar. The exterior area for the fish contains a dozen stalls and the entire establishment around one hundred. The whole of the other ground part is for the sale of butcher meat. The upper part for the same of poultry, tripe, vegetables and fruit, with one or two stalls for the sale of cured tongues, sausages and other savoury fare.'

Yet the market was not the commercial success Carnegie and his investors had hoped. There were complaints about ventilation and a planned expansion never happened. The commercial disappointment was alluded to in Captain Carnegie's obituary in 1846: 'His active mind suggested, in 1825, the erection of the new markets at Stockbridge, which now remain a splendid monument of his taste and public spirit, although, unfortunately, they have not turned out so advantageous as was at first anticipated.'

In the 1850s part of the market was moved to allow new houses to be constructed and some of the trade moved away, although butchers continued to sell from there until it finally closed in 1900. In 1903 the site – 98 feet by 57 - was advertised for sale, and in 1930 the site again was on the market, along with four tenements in St Stephen Place and two shops and two houses in St Stephen Street, at a combined price of £2,500.

WORKING MEN'S HOUSES.

A meeting was held last night for the purpose
of hearing an address by the Rev. Dr Begg on the
means to be adopted for obtaining ground for the
building of working men's houses. The chair
was occupied by Mr David Rintoul; and there
was a large attendance of working men.

The CHAIRMAN, in opening the proceedings,
referred to the suggestions contained in the last
report of the Co-operative Building Society on the
subject for which the meeting had been called—
viz., an appeal to the legislation and a sustained
agitation among the working men themselves.
In regard to the latter suggestion, it had been
said that they should not fall back upon agitation,
which would be a retrograde movement.
This, he thought, would depend entirely
upon the spirit in which such an agitation
would be conducted. He believed that this,
the age of the co-operation, was in itself
a proof that working men had now seen a
better way in which to accomplish their object
than the adoption of any wild schemes—(applause). He thought it was the duty of every
working man to do all that in him lay for the
removal of difficulties, and for the carrying out
of the object which they had at heart—(applause).

1. Ex-officials of the Edinburgh & Northern District Co-operative Society (John Dawson
- top left & David Rintoul - middle row, second left), c.1880
2. Advert for John Dawson, 1870
3. Meeting of the Cooperative Building Society chaired by David Rintoul, 1863
4. St Cuthbert's Co-operative Association butcher's shop, 1900

111

Edinburgh & Northern District Co-operative Society

The first Co-operative Society was established in Rochdale in 1844, creating a model of a business owned and controlled by its members, all of whom received a dividend from the profits. In 1859 a number of workmen in the south-west of Edinburgh set up St Cuthbert's Co-operative Association, as they felt city merchants were offering poor choice for high prices and the 83 members opened their first grocery shop on the corner of Ponton Street and Fountainbridge. After initial difficulties the Ponton Street shop began to make a profit and the committee opened a second shop at 43 Brunswick Street in June 1863. Although sales grew, there were local complaints of too high prices and poor management, and in 1866 the shop closed.

A number of local Stockbridge members, including John Dawson, a bell hanger and maker of Venetian blinds in St Stephen Street, decided to set up their own society, the Edinburgh & Northern District Co-operative Society, and re-opened the shop. In the first two years trading was poor, not helped by a significant number of members failing to pay their shop bills. To add to the fragile financial situation an unexpected expenditure arose. The store cat had met up with two other cats and in a consequent fight, a neighbour's window was damaged and she demanded compensation. The committee, having carefully considered the affair, decided that as there were three cats present when the damage was done, the store cat was only responsible for one-third of the damage and paid that share.

To survive, staff numbers were reduced and members of the committee served in the store in the evenings. The chair, David Rintoul, a mason, personally visited houses in the area promoting the benefits of the society and the financial situation improved. The commitment of the committee was remarkable. Having moved the shop to number 34 it was decided to enlarge it and one public holiday the committee members carried out all the work, with those that were not joiners or masons acting as labourers. By 1875 the society operated a bakehouse and stocked a wider selection of items, including coal, and boots and shoes. The humble hand barrow that had been the means of delivery up till then was replaced by a pony and van. There was even a co-operative marriage as Mr. Lorimer, the shop manager wed Miss McInnes, the bookkeeper.

The committee became active in the wider co-operative movement, joining the Scottish Co-operative Wholesale Society and becoming agents for the Co-operative Insurance Society. They also took shares in the Edinburgh Co-operative Printing Company and Paisley Manufacturing Society. In 1880 the success of the society – in that year the 406 members received an annual dividend of 2s6d - enabled it to purchase the whole

COMMITTEE, EDINBURGH NORTHERN DISTRICT—AUGUST 1899

Back Row—WILLIAM HARDING, WILLIAM SIME, ROBERT BRYCE
Middle Row—R. FARMER, ADAM GLEN, WILLIAM CRAWFORD, BARCLAY TODD, JAMES LAW, JOHN DUNSMORE
(Treasurer)   (President)   (Secretary)   (Manager)
Front Row—JOHN CLUNIE, C. W. MACPHERSON, ANDREW ROXBURGH, JAMES BROWN, ALEXANDER MARTIN

1. Committee of Edinburgh & Northern District Co-operative Society (Barclay Todd, Middle Row, 3rd from right), 1900
2. Banner of Raeburn Branch of Scottish Co-operative Women's Guild , 1926
3. Co-operative store in Hamilton Place (now Scotmid), 1908

113

tenement in which the store was housed for £1,350, plus a stable behind for the pony. A penny bank was launched and a draper's department opened. Improved benefits for employees were introduced and a charity fund created. The adjoining shop was purchased to enlarge the drapery department and open a tailoring and dressmaking section. By 1886 the store was the largest shop in the area.

For a time a breakaway group formed the St Bernard's Co-op but the two later re-merged. The Edinburgh & Northern Co-op opened grocery and butchers shops in Rose Street and Picardy Place, and in 1894 purchased property in Patriot Hall for £14,000. This area to the north of Brunswick Street contained bleaching works and a block of forty-three houses erected by Thomas Sprott as 'dwelling places for artisans.' There the society erected a new building containing a large bakery and a laundry. Insurance schemes for horses and for glass were introduced, and the committee helped establish a local branch of the Scottish Co-operative Women's Guild and provided premises for the fifty women members to meet. The co-op regularly supplied poor children with boots; in 1909 it donated 548 pairs.

In 1899 the then president, Barclay Todd, led an amalgamation with St. Cuthbert's Co-operative Association and the St Stephen Street store closed in 1902. The drapery and boot departments moved to Patriots Hall and the other departments moved to a new store in Hamilton Place (still a Co-op store). The Co-op's St Stephen Street building was purchased by William Green & Sons, law publishers. It was used as the firm's store through to the 1930s and then became a furniture store. The various amalgamations meant that by 1909 St Cuthbert's had become the largest co-operative in Scotland and had the highest sales of any co-op in the UK, paying out over £3.6 million in dividends to its members.

St Cuthert's
Cooperative delivery
van, c.1910

1. Duncanson's Pawnbrokers (Stockbridge Equitable Loan Company) at 10 St Stephen Street, c.1960s
2. Duncanson's premises at 23 North West Circus Place, c.1980s

Pawnbroker

In 1863 John White moved his pawnbroker business from Dean Street to 6 Brunswick Street (renumbered 10 St Stephen Street) and called it The Stockbridge Equitable Loan Company: 'Advances money on gold and silver watches, silks, tweeds, wearing apparel, instruments, tools, furniture, and every article of value.' He lived there and used one room to receive those wishing to pledge items in exchange for cash or retrieve previously pledged items. He probably stored pledged items in the basement, advertising that he had a fireproof safe for valuable items.

He had no shortage of local customers, for pawning items was the only way many could make ends meet. It was common for people to pledge their best Sunday church clothes on a Monday and redeem them on the Friday or Saturday when they had been paid. Of course, the cash lent was significantly less than an item's value. Varying rates of high interest were charged – between 15% and 30% - and there was the option of a fee for special storage, such as hanging clothes to prevent creasing. Items under 10s value not redeemed within the specified time became the pawnbroker's property, while more expensive unredeemed pledges were sold by public auction.

Stolen goods were often pawned: 'Susan Colville, a woman of no fixed residence, was sent to prison for ten days for stealing a tweed waistcoat from off a clothes line in North West Circus Place. The item was missed and afterwards pledged in a pawnbroker's in St Stephen Street by the accused, who got drunk on the proceeds.' In 1876 White was fined for having 'taken articles from a child under twelve years of age, and failed to give a ticket in the form required by the Pawnbrokers Act 1872'. No doubt the police suspected White of knowingly accepting stolen goods but unable to prove it, charged him with this offence as a warning.

James Miller Dobbie was the manager in the 1890s and had a sideline breeding and selling dogs: 'For sale that grand young English terrier bitch, "Silver Sheen", winner 1st prize Dunfermline. Also grand young black and white terrier dog, winner 3rd prize last week at Crufts, London. In splendid health; price moderate. Dobbie, 10 St Stephen Street.'

The business expanded and by the 1920s was owned by Andrew Duncanson and was situated in various properties in the street and N. W. Circus Place. Its three traditional pawnbroker's signs remain: above number 10, on the corner above The Bailie bar and above 23/24 N. W. Circus Place. By the 1950s many of the forfeited pledged items being auctioned off were of quite a different calibre to earlier days and included gold Albert chains, diamond and sapphire rings, and mink and other fur coats'. Later the firm became Duncanson & Edwards with premises in Queen Street, where it remained until closing in 2020.

1. Sandra Purves in the Lamp Emporium, 1991 (photo - Peter Stubbs)
2, Bill Purves outside the Lamp Emporium at number 59 with the ill-fated cart, 1991
(photo - Peter Stubbs)
3. Bill Purves and the restored Jowett van, 1986
4. Promotional postcard
5. An original Edinburgh streetlamp

Mr & Mrs Purves Lamp Emporium

After studying in London, where he met Sandra, Bill returned in 1970 to Edinburgh and Scotland Street. Sandra was working as a civil engineer and as Bill had to care for his father, he was looking for a job that would be flexible. They heard that Mrs Wood who owned a general store at number 59 was retiring and so arranged to buy the shop. After reflooring the shop, they then had to decide what to sell.

Across the street was the Antique Market and there, and elsewhere, Bill began to buy old oil lamps. He also bought new oil lamps, accessories and glass shades, thus launching, more by chance than design, the Purves Lamp Emporium. The business was given a boost during the power cuts from January to March 1974 that were caused by the coal miner's strike. Companies and homes had to limit their electricity usage to three consecutive days a week, and even within that span hours were severely limited. So with oil lamps being safer – and brighter – than candles, many firms and individuals became eager customers.

Bill's creative flair led him to restore the Victorian shop front and it became an influential symbol of the street's new life, and over its fifty years Purves Lamp Emporium has featured in media articles and been photographed thousands of times; and continues to delight. The shop had two modes of transportation. One was a barrow that was more decorative than functional, but suffered from a series of thefts, each time being found abandoned in the Water of Leith. Sadly, it never recovered from its third immersion. As Bill and Sandra shared a passionate interest in classic cars, they took on the daunting task of restoring a rundown 1947 Jowett van. Their skills saw it re-emerge gleaming and road-worthy, and after its many years as the shop van, currently is on display at Dundee Museum of Transport.

Sandra recounts how, before the street was made one-way, a regular amusement for those working there was instances of two vehicles converging from opposite directions. Finding themselves unable to pass, the drivers had to determine who would give way, with one having to reverse up the narrow street between the cars parked on both sides; usually after a heated exchange.

Bill died in 2016. Sandra retains the shop and opens it most Saturday afternoons. Given their shared passion for the technology of the past, it is appropriate that the recently installed replica streetlamps in Scotland Street are based on a glass globe that came from one of the street's original Georgian lamps that Bill found and preserved.

On Saturday afternoon a fire occurred in the premises of Mr James Lauriston, basket maker, 8 Brunswick Street. It seems that some baskets were being put through the process of smoking by brimstone when the wooden supports on which the baskets were set caught fire. The flames extended to the baskets themselves, but were extinguished before much damage was done. The smoke caused by the brimstone, however, caused some alarm. The High Street and Stockbridge Fire Divisions were in attendance.'

The shop at number 8 over the years (the frontage and railings probably altered when the buildings on the south side were refurbished in the late 1970s)

1. General Store, c.1920
2. Antique Shop, c.1980
3. UnKnown Italy, 2022
4. Report of fire at basket maker's shop, 1879
5. Dozo, 1972

1. VoxBox Music at number 24 & The Brotique at number 26, 2012
2. Advert for Bear Essentials at number 12, 1989
3. Interior of The Gramophone Emporium at number 21, 2014 (Capital Collection, photo – Kevin MacLean)
4. Advert for Montresor at number 35, 1993
5. Bells Diner at number 7

A flourishing future

Thankfully, St Stephen Street has survived and flourishes today. As one tourism website commented: 'St Stephen Street is perhaps Edinburgh's best-known street for independent shops. It's a peaceful spot but filled with local businesses that make it worth a visit. If you feel like treating yourself, you will love this street!'

The community of St Stephen Street photographed in 1973 for an article in the
Edinburgh Evening News

Index

Other books on Edinburgh's history by Barclay Price

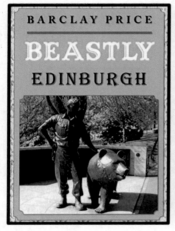
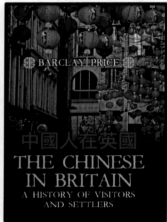

Published by Amberley Books (available from bookshops, on-line book sellers or from Amberley: https://www.amberley-books.com/

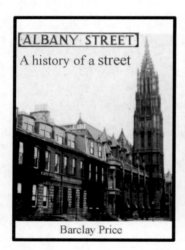
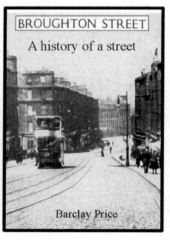

Self-published Albany Street history available from Magnum Bar, Albany Street
Broughton Street history available from Broughton Street shops: Vino Wine, Mathers Bar and Dragonfly.
Or to order, email: *albanystreetedinburgh@gmail.com*